DATE DUE

OCT 28 1990   BIRD

OCT 28 REC'D

APR BIRD

NOV 09 1992   OCT 19 1995

Y0-DSK-965

HOMICIDE IN AN URBAN COMMUNITY

HOMICIDE IN AN URBAN COMMUNITY

By

ROBERT C. BENSING, LL.B., LL.M., J.S.D.
Professor of Law
Western Reserve University
Cleveland, Ohio

and

OLIVER SCHROEDER, JR., LL.B.
Professor of Law
Director, The Law-Medicine Center
Western Reserve University
Cleveland, Ohio

With an Introductory Section by
HONORABLE PERRY B. JACKSON
Judge, Municipal Court
City of Cleveland, Ohio

CHARLES C THOMAS • PUBLISHER
Springfield · Illinois · U.S.A.

CHARLES C THOMAS · PUBLISHER
BANNERSTONE HOUSE
301-327 East Lawrence Avenue, Springfield, Illinois, U.S.A.

Published simultaneously in the British Commonwealth of Nations by
BLACKWELL SCIENTIFIC PUBLICATIONS, LTD., OXFORD, ENGLAND

Published simultaneously in Canada by
THE RYERSON PRESS, TORONTO

This book is protected by copyright. No part of it may be reproduced in any manner without written permission from the publisher.

© *1960, by* CHARLES C THOMAS · PUBLISHER

Library of Congress Catalog Card Number: 60-11259

With THOMAS BOOKS careful attention is given to all details of manufacturing and design. It is the Publisher's desire to present books that are satisfactory as to their physical qualities and artistic possibilities and appropriate for their particular use. THOMAS BOOKS will be true to those laws of quality that assure a good name and good will.

Printed in the United States of America

FOREWORD

This publication represents several years' study in depth on an ancient human problem—man's slaying man. The control period of 1947-1953 represents the best time segment for the complex legal and social aspects of the problem in an urban, industrial community. Some questions are answered; more are raised. The need for a second phase of this study is obvious. The volatile movement of people within the control community of Greater Cleveland in the past decade will provide sounder comparisons and better answers. The most which this publication can offer is a beginning for even deeper and broader research on this challenging problem of homicide—its elemental facts, its causes, and perhaps even its prevention.

ROBERT C. BENSING
OLIVER SCHROEDER, JR.

Cleveland, Ohio

SOME OPENING THOUGHTS

This study of homicide in Cuyahoga County (Greater Cleveland), Ohio is an excellent contribution for both its "legal" and "social" aspects.

The statistics of felonious homicides in Cuyahoga County over a seven year period (1947-1953) indicate that an unusually high percentage of the assailants were Negroes—76.4 percent. The rest were whites. This percentage is so much greater than the percentage of Negroes in the whole population that it very naturally raises questions as to the cause of the disparity.

But before discussing the cause or causes, it is interesting to note that there appears to be no evidence of discrimination by courts in the matter of convictions and acquittals or recommendations of mercy nor in disposition after conviction.

An analysis of the locations where the assailants lived shows the highest rates of homicides exist generally in those areas where there are the greatest social need and maladjustment. These areas correspond quite generally to areas where Negroes live in large numbers.

Perhaps the most significant feature is the fact that in the areas where Negroes, with higher economic status, higher education, higher percentage of home occupancy live, the homicide rate shows a sharp decrease from the areas where the residents are in large numbers and where public dependency, poor health, and substandard housing and monthly rental-occupied homes also predominate.

Negroes charged with felonious homicide in the majority of instances killed members of their own race. But since crime like health knows no racial barriers and since homicides contribute to create dependents of deceased victims who require public assistance, it would seem that a great challenge is prescribed for the entire community to seek to reduce substantially the social ills and needs which nurture felonious homicide.

This study should prove of unmistakable value to law enforce-

HOMICIDE IN AN URBAN COMMUNITY

ment agencies including police courts and probation officers and likewise to the Chambers of Commerce, organized labor and all other civic forces in urban areas.

Aside from those homicides which were in conjunction with another felony such as robbery, rape, burglary, etc., our own observation in the courts is that the circumstances igniting homicides in the majority of cases are trivial. Such things as anger over nonpayment of a loan of small amounts, even as low as fifty cents, jealousy, arguments while under the influence of intoxicating beverages, minor disputes of an inconsequential character in which tempers flare, predominate.

These suggest a certain amount of immaturity—the kind that results from a low economic status and very little education—a minimum of self discipline. Along with this is a noticeable lack of profitable use of leisure time. Many of the homicides occur in or near drinking or gambling establishments and other non-uplifting or non-cultural places. Other homicides are found where persons are cooped up in over-crowded housing.

We have had the opportunity also to observe the circumstances which bring white persons from the mountains of West Virginia, Kentucky or Tennessee with no previous urban experience and little or no education. Here, too, many of the same circumstances incite homicides and other crimes of violence.

We come then to some of the conclusions suggested above, that elimination of poor and over-crowded housing, increase in opportunities for employment without discrimination on the basis of race, higher education, better use of leisure time along with a decrease in other social ills will have direct bearing on the reduction of felonious homicides of Negroes in urban communities and thereby contribute to the general welfare of the community.

This challenge confronts the entire community regardless of class, creed or race.

Honorable PERRY B. JACKSON
Judge, Municipal Court
City of Cleveland, Ohio

ACKNOWLEDGMENTS

The authors express their sincere appreciation to the following whose labors, advice and cooperation made this research project and publication possible:

William B. Goldfarb

George W. O'Connor

William T. Smith

Virginia K. White

Samuel R. Gerber, M.D., Cuyahoga County Coroner
and his staff

Frank W. Story, Chief, and the Cleveland Police
Department

The late Frank T. Cullitan, Cuyahoga County Prosecutor
and his staff

The Cleveland Foundation

The Cleveland Press

R.C.B.

O.S.

CONTENTS

Page

Foreword . . . . **v**

Some Opening Thoughts vii

Acknowledgments ix

LEGAL ASPECTS OF URBAN HOMICIDE

Introduction 5

Chapter

I. Disposition of Felonious Homicides 14

II. Disposition of Specific Felonious Homicides 21

III. Races of Persons Accused of Felonious Homicides 41

IV. Females Accused of Felonious Homicides 57

V. Males Accused of Feloniously Slaying Females 64

VI. Ages of Persons Charged with Felonious Homicides . . . 70

VII. Types of Conflicts Culminating in Felonious Homicides . 72

VIII. Justifiable Homicides 78

IX. Methods Used to Slay Victims 83

X. Alcohol Statistics 92

XI. Summary 98

SOCIAL ASPECTS OF URBAN HOMICIDE

Introduction 103

Chapter

I. The Distribution of Homicide 105

II. Socio-Economic Conditions 119

xii   *HOMICIDE IN AN URBAN COMMUNITY*

                                                                    Page

III.   The Homicide Rate and Other Social Indicators 158

IV.   The Three Highest Homicide Areas Compared   177

 V.   Summary 181

Appendix A: The Census Tracts Included in the Social Planning

              Areas of Cuyahoga County 187

Index 191

HOMICIDE IN AN URBAN COMMUNITY

LEGAL ASPECTS OF URBAN HOMICIDE

INTRODUCTION: NUMBER AND CLASSIFICATION OF HOMICIDES 1947-1953

A total of 662 homicides occurred in the urban area of Greater Cleveland, Cuyahoga County, Ohio, between January 1, 1947 and December 31, 1953.[1] Traffic fatalities of an unintentional nature[2] and accidental killings where the slayer was engaged in a lawful act and, without criminal negligence, killed another[3] are not included in this total.

One hundred fifty-seven of these cases were officially ruled justifiable homicides: the intentional killing of a human being without evil design for which no legal penalty attaches.[4]

TABLE I

NUMBER OF VICTIMS AND CLASSIFICATION OF HOMICIDES
1947-1953

I. Number Ruled Justifiable Homicides		157
II. Number Unclassified Homicides		51
a. Death of slayer before charges preferred	26	
b. Number of unsolved cases	23	
c. Slayer insane; no charges preferred	1	
d. Refusal of deceased's family to prosecute	1	
III. Felonious Homicides—Charges Preferred		454
Total		662

[1]Of the total 662 homicides, 636 occurred within the City of Cleveland, and only 26, or 3.9 percent, occurred outside the City.

[2]The unlawful and unintentional killing of a person while the offender is engaged in the violation of any law of the state of Ohio applying to the use or regulation of traffic, constitutes manslaughter in the second degree. Ohio Rev. Code section 4511.18.

[3]Cases of this type fall within the common law definition of *homicide per infortunium,* a species of excusable homicide, for which there is no penalty. See BLACK'S LAW DICTIONARY (3d ed. 1933).

[4]For the purposes of this study, justifiable homicide is defined as the intentional

$\ggg\!\!\rightarrow$

6 HOMICIDE IN AN URBAN COMMUNITY

In the cases of 26 decedents, their slayers either committed suicide or died from other causes before charges could be placed against them.[5] These cases clearly come within the definition of homicide as it is defined in this study. However, an attempt to state which of these cases were justifiable and which were felonious homicides—and if the latter, whether they constituted first or second degree murder or manslaughter—would be sheer speculation.

Twenty-three cases are unsolved. These are cases in which the identities of the slayers are unknown. And again, while the evidence indicates that these are, *prima facie*, cases of either justifiable or felonious homicides, specific classifications cannot be made.

In one other case an inmate of the Lima State Hospital for the Criminally Insane killed another inmate. No charges were filed against the already committed slayer. In another instance the relatives of the victim refused to prefer charges against the assailant, so no formal legal action was instituted.

These *unclassified homicides* number 51.

Four hundred fifty-four cases now remain in which the alleged slayers were formally charged[6] with either murder in the first or

---

killing of a human being without any evil design, and under such circumstances of necessity or duty as render the act proper; such as self-defense, or where the killing takes place in an endeavor to prevent the commission of a felony which could not otherwise be avoided. BLACK'S LAW DICTIONARY (3d ed. 1933).

This definition includes *homicide se defendendo,* or in self-defense, upon a sudden affray—where one necessarily kills another, after becoming engaged in a sudden affray, in order to save himself from reasonably apparent danger of death or great bodily harm. Definition is from Clark and Marshall, LAW OF CRIMES, Sec. 273 (5th ed. 1952). Under the common law, this was classified as excusable homicide and not as justifiable homicide. For simplicity, this survey classifies as justifiable all homicides which under the common law would be defined as justifiable and those which would be defined as *homicide se defendendo,* which latter was a species of excusable homicide. The survey definition does not, however, include *homicide per infortunium,* which was the second species of excusable homicide at common law. See *supra* note 3, and text, for definition of *homicide per infortunium.*

[5]Eighteen slayers (who killed 20 persons) committed suicide; one was killed by police officers; the cause of death of one slayer is not known; and in two separate instances (involving a total of four parties), the parties killed each other.

[6]As used throughout the survey, "formally charged" means that a warrant for the arrest of the accused assailant was issued; or, if the accused was taken into custody before a warrant was obtained, that a complaint pursuant to Ohio Revised Code section 2935.05 or 2935.06 was filed before a court or magistrate; or that a bill of indictment was presented by the county prosecutor to the grand jury.

HOMICIDE IN AN URBAN COMMUNITY 7

second degrees, or with manslaughter in the first degree. These are the *felonious homicides.*[7]

NUMBER OF HOMICIDES PER YEAR

Table 2 shows the number of homicides occurring each year during this seven year period.[8] The average for the period is approximately 95 homicides per year, with a range from a low of 84 deaths in 1950 to a high of 106 in 1952.

TABLE 2

NUMBER OF HOMICIDES PER YEAR 1947-1953

1947	89
1948	97
1949	94
1950	84
1951	94
1952	106
1953	98
Total	662

NUMBER OF HOMICIDES PER MONTH 1947-1953

The average number of homicides per month for the seven year period is 55.2 per month. As indicated by Table 3, the lowest number for any month, 35 or 5.3 percent, occurred in March; while the largest number, 74 deaths or 11.2 percent, occurred in August.[9]

Upon the basis of the highest consecutive three month total, the months of July, August, and September led all others with 204 homicides, which constituted approximately 31 percent of the deaths during this period. Conversely, the lowest number of deaths

---

[7]For the penalties which may be imposed upon conviction for these felonious homicides, see pp. 21, 29, 35, *infra.*

[8]These yearly, as well as all monthly, weekly, and hourly, totals are based upon the time when the assault occurred from which death resulted, and not upon the time of death, whenever the two occurred at different times.

[9]*Ibid.*

HOMICIDE IN AN URBAN COMMUNITY

TABLE 3

VICTIMS PER MONTH
PERCENTAGE OF TOTAL
1947-1953

	Jan.	Feb.	Mar.	Apr.	May	June	July	Aug.	Sept.	Oct.	Nov.	Dec.
1947	11.2	6.7	4.5	7.9	9.0	5.6	7.9	14.6	6.7	10.1	11.2	4.5
1948	9.3	10.3	7.2	8.2	7.2	5.2	8.2	11.3	11.3	6.2	8.2	7.2
1949	9.6	5.3	6.4	7.4	11.7	9.6	7.4	10.6	7.4	6.4	6.4	11.7
1950	7.1	4.8	2.4	7.1	10.7	7.1	11.9	7.1	15.5	6.0	13.1	7.1
1951	4.3	8.5	4.3	5.3	7.4	5.3	10.6	16.0	8.5	7.4	11.7	10.6
1952	8.5	7.5	5.7	6.6	14.2	7.5	3.8	6.6	12.3	8.5	7.5	11.3
1953	5.1	6.1	6.1	5.1	9.1	4.0	16.2	12.1	10.1	8.1	7.1	11.1
Total	7.8	7.1	5.3	6.8	10.0	6.3	9.4	11.2	10.3	7.6	9.2	9.1

in any three month period—a total of 127—occurred in February, March, and April. These months, therefore, accounted for only 19.2 percent of the homicides between 1947 and 1953.

An examination of the number of cases occurring per month in the individual years which make up the totals for this seven year period, however, displays a clearer picture than that portrayed by Table 3. As seen by an analysis of Graph 1, the year-to-year fluctuations for any given month are, on the whole, too great over the seven years for the monthly totals to indicate trends of any significance.

It is believed, therefore, that these totals cannot be used as a basis for accurate prediction of future homicides.

DAYS ON WHICH ASSAULTS OCCURRED 1947-1953

Of 652 homicides,[10] the greatest number, 176 or 27 percent, occurred on Saturday. Sunday, with 128 assaults, and Friday, with

---

[10]In ten of the total 662 cases, the days on which the assaults occurred are not known.

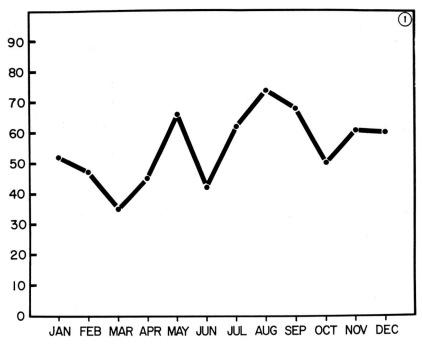

Graph 1. Number of Victims per Month 1947-1953.

TABLE 4

Days on Which 652 Assaults Occurred
Percentage of Total

	Mon.	Tues.	Wed.	Thurs.	Fri.	Sat.	Sun.
1947	10.2	9.1	5.7	12.5	19.3	20.4	23.9
1948	8.6	4.3	11.8	15.1	20.4	23.6	16.1
1949	12.9	14.0	5.4	8.6	16.1	18.3	24.7
1950	6.2	6.2	6.2	13.8	11.2	35.0	21.2
1951	6.4	10.8	7.5	11.8	12.9	33.3	17.2
1952	10.4	9.4	13.2	10.4	14.1	27.4	15.1
1953	5.1	8.1	11.1	9.1	15.2	31.3	20.2
Total	8.6	8.9	8.9	11.3	15.6	27.0	19.6

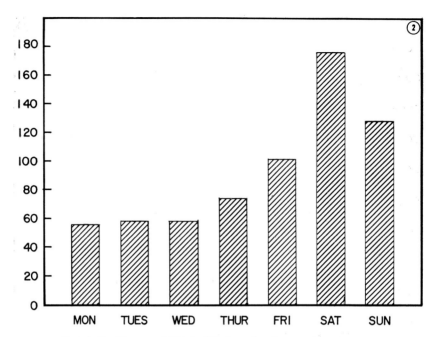

Graph 2. Days on Which 652 Assaults Occurred 1947-1953.

102, accounted for the next highest totals. The total for all three of these days amounts to 62.3 percent of the cases for the seven year period. Thursday, with 74 deaths or 11.3 percent, was the fourth highest.

Monday, with 56 homicides, and Tuesday and Wednesday, with 58 each, accounted for the least number of deaths; the combined total for these three days amounting to only 26.4 percent of all homicides for the period surveyed.

The reasons why Fridays, Saturdays, and Sundays overshadowed all other days of the week are apparent. Leisure time is greatest on these days. Fridays and Saturdays are traditional pay days. Money and leisure increase the number of social contacts. As a result, the chance of personal violence is greater.[11] In addition, money and leisure time are conducive to the drinking of alcohol which also increases the chance of violence.

---

[11] Elliott and Merrill, SOCIAL DISORGANIZATION 187 (1941).

HOURS IN WHICH ASSAULTS OCCURRED 1947-1953

Graph 3 shows in three hour periods the hours when the assaults[12] occurred in 622 homicides.[13]

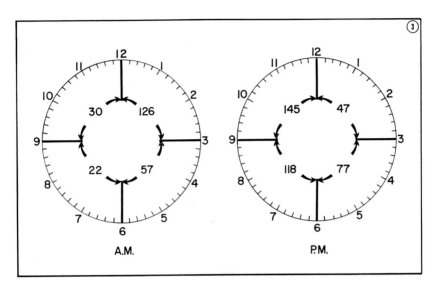

Graph 3. Hours of Assaults in 622 Cases 1947-1953.

Starting with the period of 12:01 P.M. to 3:00 P.M., in which 7.6 percent of the homicides took place, the percentage rises steadily to 19 percent between 6:01 P.M. and 9:00 P.M.; and then reaches a peak of 23.3 percent in the hours of 9:01 P.M. to midnight. From this high point, the percentage dips to 20.2 percent during 12:01 A.M. to 3:00 A.M. It then drops sharply to 9.2 percent between the hours of 3:01 A.M. and 6:00 A.M., from which point it further declines to a low of 3.5 percent in the 6:01 A.M. to 9:00 A.M. period.

The most significant fact is that 62.5 percent of all assaults took place between the hours of 6:01 P.M. and three o'clock in the morning. Again, it is to be noted that the greatest percentage of

---
[12]See *supra* note 8.
[13]In 40 cases of the total 662 cases, the times of the assaults are not known. In instances where the time of the assault or death was estimated, or where there was conflicting evidence in regard thereto, the case was recorded as "time unknown."

HOMICIDE IN AN URBAN COMMUNITY

cases occurred during a period of time which is one of leisure for most persons.

APPREHENSION OF THE ASSAILANTS—THE ROLE OF THE POLICE

In 35 cases of justifiable homicide the decedents were slain by police officers. These slayings were reported immediately, and the officers were thereafter available for arrest in the event the killings were believed felonious. Therefore, since these cases did not involve any real effort on the part of the police, as to either the identities or the apprehension of the slayers, they must be subtracted from the total number of homicides (662) for the seven year period if an accurate picture of the role of the police is to be obtained.

It is also believed that all cases in which the assailants committed suicide, or died other than at the hands of the police before charges could be formally placed against them should be excluded. Twenty-five cases are within this classification.

With the elimination of the above 60 cases from the total, the remaining 602 homicides fall within the following categories:

Justifiable homicides (assailants not police officers)	122
Unsolved homicides (identities of assailants unknown)	23
Assailant killed by police before charges filed	1
Assailants apprehended but charges not filed[14]	2
Felonious homicides (assailants not apprehended— charges filed)[15]	4
Felonious homicides—slayers arrested and charges filed	450
Total	602

Thus, the police of Cuyahoga County have apprehended the assailants, or the persons whom they believed to be the assailants,

---

[14]In one of these cases the slayer was an officially-committed inmate of the Lima State Hospital for the insane. In the other, the relatives of the deceased refused to prefer charges against the slayer, and no legal action was instituted.

[15]The identities of these slayers are known, and warrants for their arrest, charging them with the commission of felonious homicides, have been issued. Not included in this total of four cases is one case in which the slayer is in prison in another state. A warrant for his arrest is on file.

HOMICIDE IN AN URBAN COMMUNITY

in all but 27, or 4.5 percent, of the 602 homicides occurring in the seven year period surveyed.[16] A truly remarkable record!

---

[16]Even if all cases of justifiable homicide, police (35 cases) and non-police (122 cases), are subtracted from the total 622, and if the cases in which the slayers committed suicide or died other than at the hands of the police before charges could be placed against them, are also subtracted (25 cases), the police still apprehended all but 5.6 percent of the assailants during the period surveyed.

Chapter I

DISPOSITION OF FELONIOUS HOMICIDES — A CONSIDERATION OF THE STATISTICS AS AN INTEGRATED WHOLE 1947-1953

Table 5 shows the disposition of the cases of 462 persons officially charged with feloniously killing 454 persons during the period surveyed.

Of these 462 alleged slayers, five have not been apprehended.[17] Two cases were still pending at the time of writing; two defendants died before they could be brought to trial; and the disposition of three cases is unknown.

The disposition of the remaining 450 cases is shown in Table 5.

ACCUSED DISCHARGED UPON PRELIMINARY EXAMINATION

When a person is arrested for a felonious homicide in Ohio, a preliminary examination is held before a municipal court or a magistrate unless the accused waives his right to the examination.[18] If the examination is waived, or if the court or magistrate finds that an offense has been committed, and that there is probable cause to believe the accused guilty, the prisoner is "bound over" to the grand jury. Conversely, if upon preliminary examination it is found that an offense has not been committed, or that there is no probable cause for believing the accused guilty, he is discharged.

Fifteen accused slayers were discharged upon preliminary examination.

---

[17]One of these accused slayers is presently in jail in another state.
[18]See Ohio Revised Code sections 2937.01-2937.12.

HOMICIDE IN AN URBAN COMMUNITY

TABLE 5

DISPOSITION OF FELONIOUS HOMICIDES
1947-1953

Part I

I. Number convicted as charged by indictment	99
a. Pleaded guilty — 24	
b. Found guilty — 75	
1. By court — 29	
2. By jury — 44	
3. Unknown — 2	
II. Number convicted of lesser offenses	171
a. Pleaded guilty — 87	
b. Found guilty — 84	
1. By court — 28	
2. By jury — 56	
III. Not guilty	106
1. By court — 43	
2. By jury — 63	
IV. Insane at time of trial	16
V. Not guilty by reason of insanity	1
VI. Nolle prosequis	1
VII. "No Bill" by grand jury	41
VIII. Discharged upon preliminary examination	15
Total	450

Part II

I. Abated by death of accused before trial	2
II. Accused not apprehended	5
a. Whereabouts unknown — 4	
b. Accused in jail in another state — 1	
III. Trial of case pending	2
IV. Disposition of case unknown	3
Total	12
Combined Total	462

FAILURE OF GRAND JURY TO INDICT

After preliminary examination if the accused is "bound over" to the grand jury, the county prosecutor then presents the evidence in the case to that body. However, neither the arrest of the accused slayer nor a preliminary examination is necessary. Evidence may be, and sometimes is, presented directly to the grand jury by the prosecutor without prior proceedings of any type against the accused.

In either event, if after considering the evidence the grand jury believes the case should be tried, they return a "true bill of indictment." This states the offense for which the accused is indicted. If the grand jury fails to indict, they return what is ordinarily referred to as a "no bill." The latter return operates as a discharge of the proceedings against the accused, and results in his release if he has been held in custody.

Forty-one cases were "no-billed" by the grand juries which sat during the seven year period of the survey. Excluding the 15 cases in which the defendants were discharged upon preliminary examination, and the five cases in which the accused persons are unapprehended, these 41 "no billed" cases represent 9.3 percent of the cases.[19]

NOLLE PROSEQUIS

Even after indictment the prosecuting attorney may not be willing to prosecute. He may enter a motion of *nolle prosequi*[20] in the case, which, if granted by the court, results in the discharge of the accused.

Two cases were *"nolled"* during the period of 1947-1953. In one of these, however, the accused was immediately re-indicted for first-degree murder, found guilty, and electrocuted. Since the final disposition of this case was other than by *nolle prosequi,* for the pur-

---

[19]In the two cases in which the accused died before trial, and the three in which the disposition is unknown, it is not known whether indictments were returned. If these cases are also excluded, then "no bills" were returned in 9.4 percent of the cases.

[20]If a *nolle prosequi* is entered, and the motion is granted by the court before jeopardy attaches, the state is not precluded from re-indicting and trying the accused for the same offense.

poses of this study it is excluded from the category of *"nolled"* cases, and only one case is counted as falling within such classification.

ACCUSED INSANE

Under Ohio law, when a defendant is found to be insane at the time of the trial of his case, trial is postponed, and he is committed to an institution for the duration of his insanity.[21]

Sixteen defendants were found insane at the time of trial, and were committed to the Lima State Hospital for the Criminally Insane until their reason is restored. This represents 4.1 percent of the 393 cases within the first five categories listed in Table 5: Number convicted as originally charged by indictment; Number convicted of lesser offenses; Not guilty; Not guilty by reason of insanity; Insane at time of trial.

Any defendant who is sane at the time of the trial of his case must, of course, stand trial. If he was insane at the time of the commission of the alleged offense, however, he cannot be convicted of a crime. In only one case was an accused found not guilty by reason of insanity.

NOT GUILTY

With the exclusion of the one case in which the accused was found not guilty by reason of insanity, of 265 cases in which the defendants actually stood trial and the termination of the prosecution was as a result of the determination of guilt or innocence by a court or jury,[22] 106 defendants, or 40 percent, were found not guilty of any criminal offense and were discharged.

CONVICTIONS

Two hundred and seventy defendants were convicted of some

21See Ohio Revised Code sections 2945.37 *et seq*. Upon being restored to reason the accused is then proceeded against as provided by law. Ohio Revised Code section 2945.38.

22The total of 265 cases is the sum of the following: 75 cases in which the defendants were found guilty as originally charged by indictment; 84 found guilty of lesser offenses; 106 found not guilty.

18 *HOMICIDE IN AN URBAN COMMUNITY*

type of criminal offense. That is, they were either convicted as charged by indictment, or were convicted of a lesser offense.[23]

Of this number, 99 defendants, or 36.7 percent, were convicted as originally charged; and 171, or 63.3 percent, were convicted of lesser offenses.

NUMBER PLEADING GUILTY

Twenty-four, or 24.2 percent, of the 99 defendants convicted as charged by indictment were convicted on their pleas of guilty. The remaining 75 were found guilty as charged after deliberation by a court or a jury.

Of the 171 convicted of lesser offenses 87, or 50.9 percent, were convicted upon their pleas of guilty.

Thus, of the total 270 convictions for some type criminal offense, 41.1 percent of the convictions were obtained as a result of pleas of guilty.

DISPOSITION AND METHOD OF TRIAL—COURT OR JURY

Excluding one case in which the defendant was found not guilty by reason of insanity, and two cases in which the manner of trial is unknown, a total of 263 defendants were forced to elect between trial by jury or trial by court.

One hundred waived their right to trial by jury and chose to be tried by a court. Of this number: 29 percent were found guilty of the crimes for which they were indicted; 28 percent were found guilty of lesser offenses; and 43 percent were found not guilty of any offense.

Of the 163 electing trial by jury: 27 percent were found guilty as originally charged; 34.4 percent were convicted of lesser offenses; and 38.6 were found not guilty.

Appraised statistically, a defendant's chances would appear to have been about the same whichever method of trial he elected. Actually, of course, the leniency of a court or jury cannot be ap-

---

[23]Only defendants convicted of the felonious homicides for which they were originally indicted come within the category of "convicted as charged by indictment." All others fall within the category of "convicted of a lesser offense."

HOMICIDE IN AN URBAN COMMUNITY 19

praised statistically, for one must be acquainted with the facts in each case, and even then reasonable minds may differ.

TABLE 6

COMPARISON OF DISPOSITION OF CASES TRIED BY COURT AND BY JURY

A. Convicted as charged.
    a. Trial by court _____ 29%
    b. Trial by jury _____ 27%

B. Convicted of lesser offenses.
    a. Trial by court _____ 28%
    b. Trial by jury _____ 34.4%

C. Not guilty.
    a. Trial by court _____ 43%
    b. Trial by jury _____ 38.6%

PROBATION

Out of a total of 191 defendants convicted of offenses other than murder, and who were therefore eligible,[24] only 33, or 17.3 percent, received suspended sentences and were placed upon probation.

A SUMMARY OF THE STATISTICS ON CONVICTION

In summarizing the conviction statistics, it is found that of 376 defendants[25] who were either found not guilty or were convicted of some type offense: 26.3 percent were convicted as originally charged by indictment; 45.5 percent were convicted of lesser offenses; and 28.2 percent were found not guilty of any offense. Upon adding the percentages in the first two categories, the over-all conviction figure is 71.8 percent for the years studied.

If, however, the 111 cases in which the defendants either pleaded guilty as charged or pleaded guilty of lesser offenses are

---

[24]"No person convicted of murder shall be placed on probation." Ohio Revised Code section 2951.04.

[25]Not included in this total is the one case in which the accused was found not guilty by reason of insanity.

excluded, the over-all percentage of convictions drops to approximately 60 percent. And, conversely, the percentage of defendants found not guilty rises to approximately 40 percent.

Chapter II

DISPOSITION OF SPECIFIC FELONIOUS HOMICIDES

Heretofore, all cases in which the defendants were charged with murder in the first degree, murder in the second degree, or manslaughter in the first degree were combined, and discussed under the general heading of "felonious homicides." This chapter reverses this procedure, and discusses the cases in the light of the specific offenses with which the defendants were charged.

A. MURDER IN THE FIRST DEGREE

The Ohio Revised Code provides that:

> No person shall purposely, and either of deliberate and premeditated malice, or by means of poison, or in perpetrating or attempting to perpetrate rape, arson, robbery, or burglary, kill another.

And that:

> Whoever violates this section is guilty of murder in the first degree and shall be punished by death unless the jury trying the accused recommends mercy, in which case the punishment shall be imprisonment for life.[26]

Additional sections of the code also provide that: (1) death caused by the malicious placing of an obstruction upon a railroad, or the displacing or injuring anything pertaining thereto with the intent to endanger the passage of a locomotive or car;[27] (2) the killing of a guard or officer by a convict;[28] (3) and the willful and

---

[26]Ohio Revised Code section 2901.01.

[27]Ohio Revised Code section 2901.02. No cases of this type found during period surveyed.

[28]Ohio Revised Code section 2901.03. No cases of this type found during period surveyed.

intentional killing of a sheriff, deputy sheriff, constable, police-man, or marshal while such peace officer is engaged in the dis-charge of his duties,[29] constitute murder in the first degree and are punishable by death unless mercy is recommended, in which case the punishment shall be imprisonment for life.[30]

Number Charged with Murder in the First Degree

Although 462 defendants were charged with the commission of some type felonious homicide, only 116, or approximately 25 percent, were formally charged with the commission of murder in the first degree as that offense is defined in the various sections of the Ohio Revised Code.[31]

Disposition Other Than by Trial or Conviction
Upon a Plea of Guilty

Of the 116 defendants charged with first degree murder, three, or 2.6 percent, have not been apprehended. Two defendants died before trial; the trial of one case was pending at the time of writing; and in two cases the defendants were apprehended but the disposi-tion of their cases is unknown.

None of the alleged slayers was discharged upon preliminary examination, and in only four cases did the grand jury fail to return an indictment.

Twelve defendants were found to be insane at the time of trial, and were committed to the Lima State Hospital for the Criminally Insane until their reason is restored. This represents 11.5 percent

---

[29]Ohio Revised Code section 2901.04. Two cases of this type occurred during period of survey.

[30]Maliciously and willfully taking the life of the President or Vice-President of the United States, or of any person in the line of succession to the presidency under the laws of the United States, is punishable by death. Ohio Revised Code section 2901.09.

Similarly, maliciously and willfully taking the life of the governor or lieutenant governor of a state, territory, or possession of the United States is punishable by death. Ohio Revised Code section 2901.10.

In neither of the above sections, however, is the offense specifically classified as "murder in the first degree." Indeed, it is not classified at all. Abduction, or kidnap-ing resulting in death, is also first degree murder, and is punishable by death, or if mercy is recommended, by imprisonment for life. Ohio Revised Code section 2901.28.

No cases involving any of these three sections occurred during the period surveyed.

[31]See *supra* notes 26-30.

HOMICIDE IN AN URBAN COMMUNITY

TABLE 7

TOTAL CHARGED WITH MURDER IN THE FIRST DEGREE

I. Total Convicted First Degree Murder	33
(a) Pleaded Guilty — 4	
(b) Found Guilty — 29	
1) By Court — 12	
2) By Jury — 17	
(c) Mercy Recommended — 24	
1) By Court — 13	
2) By Jury — 11	
(d) Death — 9	
1) By Court — 3	
2) By Jury — 6	
II. Total Convicted of Lesser Offenses	48
A. Murder Second Degree — 30	
(a) Pleaded Guilty — 10	
(b) Found Guilty — 20	
1) By Court — 9	
2) By Jury — 11	
B. Manslaughter First Degree — 18	
(a) Pleaded Guilty — 8	
(b) Found Guilty — 10	
1) By Court — 2	
2) By Jury — 8	
III. Not Guilty	11
(1) By Court — 1	
(2) By Jury — 10	
IV. Insane at Time of Trial	12
V. Nolle Prosequis	0
VI. Not Guilty by Reason of Insanity	0
VII. Discharged upon Preliminary Examination	0
VIII. "No Bill" by Grand Jury	4
IX. Accused not Apprehended	3
X. Abated by Death of Accused before Trial	2
XI. Trial of Case Pending	1
XII. Disposition of Case Unknown	2
Total	116

24 HOMICIDE IN AN URBAN COMMUNITY

of the 104 cases in which the defendants were either convicted of some type criminal offense, found not guilty, or were insane at the time of trial.

Number Found Not Guilty

Eleven defendants tried for first degree murder were found not guilty and released. This represents 15.7 percent of the defendants indicted for murder in the first degree who actually stood trial, and who were found guilty of some offense, or not guilty, as a result of the deliberations of a court or jury.[32]

Number of Convictions

Eighty-one defendants were indicted for first degree murder and convicted of some type offense. Thirty-three, or 40.7 percent, were convicted of murder in the first degree as originally charged; 30, or 37 percent, were convicted of murder in the second degree; and 18, or 22.2 percent, were convicted of manslaughter in the first degree.

Number Pleading Guilty

Only four of the 33 persons convicted of murder in the first degree pleaded guilty. Ten of the 30 defendants convicted of murder in the second degree and eight of the 18 convicted of manslaughter in the first degree pleaded guilty, however.

Thus, while a total of 81 persons indicted for first degree murder were convicted of some crminal offense, 27.2 percent pleaded guilty to the offenses with which they were convicted.

Summary of Conviction Statistics

In summarizing the statistics on murder in the first degree, it is found that a total of 92 persons were either convicted as indicted, convicted of a lesser offense, or were found not guilty. Of this number: 35.9 percent were convicted of first degree murder; 32.6 of murder in the second degree; 19.6 of first degree manslaughter; and 12 percent were found not guilty of any offense and released.

Thus, 88 percent of the persons within the above categories were convicted of felonious homicides.

---

[32]A total of 70 defendants are within this category. See items I b., II A. (b), II B. (b), and III of Table 7.

HOMICIDE IN AN URBAN COMMUNITY

Since 22 of these defendants pleaded guilty, either as originally indicted, or to a lesser offense, if these 22 cases are subtracted from the total 92 who were either convicted or found not guilty, the over-all conviction rate drops to 84.3 percent.

Disposition and Method of Trial—Court or Jury

Of the 70 defendants indicted for first degree murder who actually stood trial, and whose guilt or innocence was determined as a result of the deliberations of a court or a jury, 24 elected to be tried by a court and 46 chose to be tried by a jury.

Twelve, or 50 percent, of the persons tried by a court were found guilty of first degree murder; nine, or 37.5 percent, were convicted of second degree murder; two, or 8.3 percent, were found guilty of manslaughter in the first degree; and only one defendant was found not guilty and released.

The cases of the 46 defendants electing trial by jury were disposed of as follows: 17, or 37 percent, were convicted of first degree murder as originally charged; 11, or 23.9 percent, were found guilty of second degree murder; eight, or 17.4 percent, were convicted of first degree manslaughter; ten, or 21.7 precent, were found not guilty and released.

TABLE 8

Murder in the First Degree—Disposition of Cases when Tried by Court or by Jury

I. Convicted of First Degree Murder.	
a) Trial by Court	50.0%
b) Trial by Jury	36.9%
II. Convicted of Second Degree Murder.	
a) Trial by Court	37.5%
b) Trial by Jury	23.9%
III. Convicted of First Degree Manslaughter.	
a) Trial by Court	8.3%
b) Trial by Jury	17.4%
IV. Found Not Guilty.	
a) Trial by Court	4.2%
b) Trial by Jury	21.7%

Thus, while 95.8 percent of those who were tried by a court were convicted of some felonious homicide, only 78.3 percent who chose trial by a jury were so convicted.

Recommendation of Mercy

With the exception of the willful and malicious killing of certain public officials,[33] where the death penalty is the only one provided for, the punishment upon conviction of murder in the first degree in Ohio is death *unless* the jury trying the accused recommends mercy,[34] in which case the punishment is imprisonment for life.[35]

Of 33 defendants convicted of murder in the first degree, mercy was extended to 24, or 72.7 percent.

Recommendation by Court or Jury

The courts extended mercy more often than did the juries. Out of a total of 16 defendants who either pleaded guilty[36] of murder in the first degree, or who waived trial by jury and were found guilty by a court, 13, or 81.2 percent, were extended mercy. Upon conviction after trial by a jury, however, mercy was recommended in only 11 of 17 cases, or 64.7 percent.

Felony Murder Statistics

In 82 of the 116 cases in which persons were charged with murder in the first degree, they were charged solely with having killed purposely and with deliberate and premeditated malice. In the remaining 34 cases the defendants were charged with two or more counts of first degree murder. They were charged in one count with having killed purposely and with deliberate and premeditated malice, and, in addition, were charged with one or more

---

[33]See *supra* note 30.

[34]Where a defendant pleads guilty to murder in the first degree, or waives trial by jury and is found guilty by the court, the court has the power to extend mercy. State v. Habig, 106 Ohio St. 151, 140 N.E. 195 (1922); State v. Lucear, 93 Ohio App. 281, 109 N.E. 2d 39 (1952).

[35]See Ohio Revised Code sections 2901.01-2901.04, 2901.28.

[36]Three of the four defendants pleading guilty to first degree murder were extended mercy by the court. The one defendant not granted mercy pleaded guilty to both premeditated murder and the felony murder of killing by means of poison. The victim was the defendant's wife.

TABLE 9

A Comparison of Premeditated Murder and Felony Murder Convictions

	Premeditated Murder First Degree	Premeditated Murder First Degree with Count of Felony Murder
Total Charged	82	34
Total convicted	11	22
Pleaded Guilty	3	1
Found Guilty After Trial	8	21
1) By Court	3	9
2) By Jury	5	12
Mercy Recommended	10	14
1) By Court	6	7
2) By Jury	4	7
Death	1	8
1) By Court	0	3
2) By Jury	1	5
Total Convicted of lesser offense	42	6
a. Murder Second	27	3
Pleaded Guilty	9	1
Found Guilty after Trial	18	2
1) By Court	9	0
2) By Jury	9	2
b. Manslaughter First	15	3
Pleaded Guilty	7	1
Found Guilty after Trial	8	2
1) By Court	2	0
2) By Jury	6	2
Not Guilty	9	2
1) By Court	1	0
2) By Jury	8	2
Nolle Prosequis	0	0
Insane at Time of Trial	12	0
Not Guilty by Reason of Insanity	0	0
Total Times Bail Granted	0	0
No Bill	1	3
Abated by Death	1	1
Not Apprehended—Warrants on File	3	0
Case Pending	1	0
Disposition Unknown	2	0

of the so-called felony murders,[37] such as intentionally killing a police officer; intentionally killing by means of poison; or intentionally killing another while perpetrating or attempting to perpetrate: arson, robbery, rape, or burglary.[38]

Twenty-two of the defendants charged with two or more counts of first degree murder were convicted of at least one of the counts. In the cases of four of these, they were convicted of both premeditated and deliberate murder as well as felony murder. In nine cases, the defendants were convicted of the felony murders with which they were charged, but were found not guilty of premeditated and deliberate murder in the first degree. In the remaining nine cases, the records disclosed only that the defendants were convicted of first degree murder. It could not be ascertained whether they had been convicted of more than one count, or if only one; and if the latter, whether it was for a felony murder or for premeditated and deliberate murder in the first degree. These 22 convictions represent 73.3 percent of the felony murder defendants who were convicted of some offense, or who were tried and found not guilty and released.[39]

In comparison, only 11 of the 82 defendants charged with the one count of deliberate and premeditated murder in the first degree were convicted of that offense. This represents only 17.7 percent of the defendants charged with such one count who were convicted of some type offense, or who were found not guilty and discharged[40] (see Table 9).

One would, of course, expect the conviction rate to be substantially higher in felony murder cases than in cases charging deliberate and premeditated murder in the first degree. In both,

---

[37]See *supra* notes 26-30, and text discussion in connection with notes.

[38]The specific felony murder charges were: killing police officers—two defendants; poison—one defendant; rape—one defendant; arson—one defendant; robbery—24 defendants; rape and robbery—four defendants; killing by poison in the commission of a robbery—one defendant.

[39]This percentage is based upon a total of 30 cases. The three cases which were "no billed" and the one abated by death are not included in this total. See Table 9.

[40]This percentage is based upon a total of 62 cases. The following are not included in this total: 12 cases in which defendants were insane at time of trial; one case abated by death; one case "no billed"; one case still pending; two cases disposition unknown. See Table 9.

HOMICIDE IN AN URBAN COMMUNITY

the killing must have been intentional. In felony murders, however, deliberate and premeditated malice is not required.[41]

Similarly, all but one of the 11 defendants charged and convicted only of the count of premeditated murder were granted mercy. Of the 22 persons charged with both premeditated murder and felony murders, and convicted of one or more of such counts, only 63.6 percent were given mercy.

Probation

None of the defendants convicted of murder in the first or second degrees received suspended sentences, for while probation is discretionary with the courts in most crimes, the Ohio Revised Code provides that: "No person convicted of murder . . . shall be placed on probation."[42]

Eighteen defendants indicted for first degree murder were convicted of manslaughter in the first degree and were, therefore, technically eligible for probation. None, however, was placed on probation.

B. MURDER IN THE SECOND DEGREE

The Ohio Revised Code provides that whoever "purposely and maliciously kills another" is guilty of murder in the second degree and shall be imprisoned for life.[43] Excluding the special cases provided for by the Ohio Code, such as killing by means of poison, killing in the perpetration of certain felonies, etc.,[44] it is the absence of the requirement of deliberate and premeditated malice which distinguishes murder in the second degree from first degree murder.[45]

Number Charged with Murder in the Second Degree

A total of 462 persons were formally charged with the commission of various felonious homicides during the period of 1947-

---

[41]Lattin, *Homicide*, 21 OHIO JURISPRUDENCE sections 9 *et seq.* (1932).

[42]Ohio Revised Code section 2951.04.

[43]Ohio Revised Code section 2901.05.

[44]See *supra* notes 26-30, and text discussion in connection with footnotes.

[45]Lattin, *Homicide*, 21 OHIO JURISPRUDENCE section 8 (1932).

TABLE 10

Murder in the Second Degree

I. Total Convicted of Second Degree Murder		16
a) Pleaded Guilty	1	
b) Found Guilty	15	
1) By Court	4	
2) By Jury	11	
II. Total Convicted of Lesser Offenses		102
A. Manslaughter First Degree	100	
a) Pleaded Guilty	57	
b) Found Guilty	43	
1) By Court	10	
2) By Jury	33	
B. Carrying Concealed Weapon	1	
a) Pleaded Guilty	0	
b) Found Guilty	1	
1) By Court	1	
2) By Jury	0	
C. Assault and Battery	1	
a) Pleaded Guilty	1	
b) Found Guilty	0	
III. Not Guilty		33
1) By Court	12	
2) By Jury	21	
IV. Insane at Time of Trial		4
V. Nolle Prosequis		0
VI. Not Guilty by Reason of Insanity		1
a) By Court	1	
VII. Discharged Upon Preliminary Examination		0
VIII. "No Bill" by Grand Jury		1
IX. Accused not Apprehended		2
a) Whereabouts Unknown	1	
b) Accused in Jail in Another State	1	
X. Trial of Case Pending		1
XI. Disposition of Case Unknown		1
Total		161

HOMICIDE IN AN URBAN COMMUNITY

1953.[46] One hundred sixty-one of these were charged with murder in the second degree.

Disposition Other Than by Trial or Upon a Plea of Guilty

Of the 161 persons charged with second degree murder: two have not been apprehended by the police of Cuyahoga County; the disposition of the case of one defendant is unknown; and the trial of one case was pending at the time of writing.

None of the persons accused of murder in the second degree was discharged upon preliminary examination; no cases were "*nolled*"; and only one case was "no billed."

Four defendants were found to be insane at the time of trial, and were committed to the Lima State Hospital for the Criminally Insane until their reason is restored.

Disposition as a Result of Trial or Upon a Plea of Guilty

In 152 cases the defendants were either convicted of murder in the second degree as charged, convicted of a lesser criminal offense, or were found not guilty.

Number Found Not Guilty

Of the total number charged with second degree murder: 93 defendants were indicted, pleaded not guilty, and were found guilty or innocent as a result of the deliberations of a court or jury.[47] Thirty-three of these 93 persons, or 35.5 percent, were found not guilty without qualification, and one defendant was found not guilty by reason of insanity at the time of the commission of the homicide.

Number of Convictions

One hundred eighteen defendants indicted for second degree murder were either convicted of that offense or were convicted of a lesser offense. Only 16, or 13.6 percent, of these 118 defendants were convicted of murder in the second degree. One hundred, or 84.7 percent, however, were convicted of manslaughter in the first

---

[46]That is, they were charged either with first degree murder, second degree murder, or manslaughter in the first degree.

[47]This classification excludes the 59 cases in which the defendants pleaded guilty as charged, or guilty of a lesser offense.

32 *HOMICIDE IN AN URBAN COMMUNITY*

degree; one was found guilty of carrying a concealed weapon;[48] and one pleaded guilty to assault and battery.[49]

Number Pleading Guilty

While only one of the persons indicted for second degree murder pleaded guilty as charged, 57 pleaded guilty to the lesser offense of manslaughter in the first degree, and one pleaded guilty to assault and battery.

Thus, while 118 defendants who were indicted for second degree murder were convicted of some offense, 59, or 50 percent, pleaded guilty to the offenses for which they were convicted.

Summary of Conviction Statistics

In summary, of the total 152 defendants who were convicted of murder in the second degree, convicted of a lesser offense, or who were found not guilty: 10.5 percent were convicted of second degree murder; 65.8 percent of manslaughter in the first degree; .6 percent (one defendant) was convicted of carrying a concealed weapon; and .6 percent (one defendant) was convicted of assault and battery. Only 33 defendants, or 21.7 percent, were found not guilty without qualification, and only one, or .6 percent, was found not guilty by reason of insanity.

Therefore, 77.6 percent of the defendants within the categories above were convicted of second degree murder or of some lesser offense. Since, however, 59 of these 152 pleaded guilty as charged, or pleaded guilty of a lesser offense, if these 59 cases are subtracted from the total 152, the over-all conviction rate drops from 77.6 percent to 63.4 percent. That is, if only the defendants who stood trial and had their guilt or innocence determined as a result of the deliberations of a court or a jury are considered, 63.4 percent were found guilty of some criminal offense.

---

[48]The penalty for carrying a concealed weapon in Ohio is a fine of not more than five hundred dollars, or imprisonment in the county jail or workhouse for not less than thirty days nor more than six months, or imprisonment in the penitentiary for not less than one nor more than three years. Ohio Revised Code section 2923.01.

[49]The penalty for assault and battery is a fine of not more than two hundred dollars or imprisonment in the county jail or workhouse for not more than six months, or both. See Ohio Revised Code sections 2901.25 and 1.05, 1.06.

HOMICIDE IN AN URBAN COMMUNITY

Disposition and Method of Trial—Court or Jury

Although 161 persons were formally charged with murder in the second degree, only 93 stood trial and were found guilty as charged, guilty of a lesser offense, or not guilty as a result of the deliberations of a court or a jury.

Of these 93 defendants, 28 elected to be tried by a court. Sixty-five chose trial by a jury.

TABLE 11

MURDER SECOND DEGREE—DISPOSITION OF CASES WHEN TRIED BY COURT OR BY JURY

I. Convicted of Second Degree Murder	
(a) Trial by Court	14.3%
(b) Trial by Jury	16.9%
II. Convicted of First Degree Manslaughter	
(a) Trial by Court	35.7%
(b) Trial by Jury	50.8%
III. Convicted of Lesser Offenses	
(a) Trial by Court	3.6%
(b) Trial by Jury	0.0%
IV. Found Not Guilty	
(a) Trial by Court	42.8%
(b) Trial by Jury	32.3%
V. Found Not Guilty by Reason of Insanity	
(a) Trial by Court	3.6%
(b) Trial by Jury	0.0%

Only four, or 14.3 percent, of the defendants tried by a court were found guilty of second degree murder; ten, or 35.7 percent, were convicted of first degree manslaughter; and one defendant was found guilty of carrying a concealed weapon. Twelve persons, or 42.8 percent, were found not guilty without qualification, and one defendant was found not guilty by reason of insanity at the time of the commission of the homicide.

The cases of the 65 defendants electing trial by a jury were disposed of as follows: 11, or 16.9 percent, were convicted as indicted of murder in the second degree; 33, or 50.8 percent, were found guilty of manslaughter in the first degree; and 21, or 32.3

34   *HOMICIDE IN AN URBAN COMMUNITY*

percent, were found not guilty without qualification and were released.

Thus, while 53.6 percent of the defendants electing trial by a court were convicted of some type criminal offense, 67.7 percent of those choosing trial by a jury were so convicted.

Probation

Since the courts are prohibited by statute[50] in Ohio from placing a defendant convicted of murder on probation, none of the persons convicted of murder in the second degree received suspended sentences.

Of the 102 defendants who were convicted of lesser offenses, however, 19, or 18.6 percent, received suspended sentences. Eighteen of these defendants had been convicted of first degree manslaughter and one had been convicted of assault and battery.

TABLE 12

DEFENDANTS INDICTED FOR MURDER SECOND DEGREE—
NUMBER OF SUSPENDED SENTENCES AND DURATION OF PROBATION

I. Manslaughter First Degree—Number of Suspended Sentences 18
   1) Duration of probation two years 14
      a) Pleaded Guilty 7
      b) Found Guilty 7
   2) Duration of Probation three years 1
      a) Found Guilty 1
   3) Duration of Probation five years 3
      a) Pleaded Guilty 2
      b) Found Guilty 1
II. Assault and Battery—Number of Suspended Sentences 1
   1) Duration of Probation two years 1
      a) Pleaded Guilty 1
              Total 19

In three instances in which defendants were convicted of first degree manslaughter, the court suspended the penitentiary sentences and placed the convicts on probation; conditioned upon

---

[50]Ohio Revised Code section 2951.04.

HOMICIDE IN AN URBAN COMMUNITY

their first serving terms in the county jail. These terms varied from ninety days in the case of one convict, to four months in the case of the second, and six months in that of the third. A commendable condition of probation was placed upon another defendant convicted of first degree manslaughter. The court required him to assist in the support of the victim's children to the best of his ability during the five year period of his probation.

C. MANSLAUGHTER IN THE FIRST DEGREE

The Ohio Revised Code provides: "No person shall unlawfully kill another," and that whoever does so is guilty of manslaughter in the first degree and shall be imprisoned not less than one nor more than twenty years.[51]

As interpreted by the courts, the offense consists of two divisions—voluntary and involuntary manslaughter. Voluntary manslaughter is defined as the unlawful and intentional killing of another while the slayer is under the influence of a sudden passion or heat of blood produced by an adequate and reasonable provocation, and before a reasonable time has elapsed for the blood to cool and reason to assume its habitual control.[52] Malice is not an element, for while the killing is unlawful and intentional, it is considered that the adequate provocation resulting in sudden passion or heat of blood has momentarily deprived the slayer of his reason; that he is impelled to act by reason of the provocation and is, therefore, without the capacity to reflect.[53] Involuntary manslaughter is the unintentional killing of another by one engaged in

---

[51]The complete statute reads: "No person shall unlawfully kill another. Whoever violates this section, except in the manner described in sections 2901.01 to 2901.05, inclusive, of the Revised Code, is guilty of manslaughter in the first degree, and shall be imprisoned not less than one nor more than twenty years." Ohio Revised Code section 2901.06.

Sections 2901.01 through 2901.04 and section 2901.28 deal with first and second degree murder. They are set forth in footnotes 26 to 30, inclusive, and note 43, *supra*, and the text discussion in connection with these notes.

[52]State v. Carter, 75 Ohio App. 545, 58 N.E. 2d 794 (1944). Also see State v. Robinson, 161 Ohio St. 213, 118 N.E. 2d 517 (1954); State v. Schaeffer, 96 Ohio St. 215, 117 N.E. 220 (1917). For an excellent discussion of the subject, see Lattin, *Homicide,* 21 OHIO JURISPRUDENCE sections 22 *et seq.* (1932).

[53]State v. Carter, 75 Ohio App. 545, 58 N.E. 2d 794 (1944).

36 *HOMICIDE IN AN URBAN COMMUNITY*

the commission of an unlawful act, which act is the proximate cause of death.[54]

Therefore, manslaughter in the first degree, whether voluntary or involuntary, is distinguishable from first degree murder: the latter requires deliberate and premeditated malice or an inten-

TABLE 13

MANSLAUGHTER IN THE FIRST DEGREE

I. Total Convicted—Manslaughter First Degree		50
a) Pleaded Guilty	19	
b) Found Guilty	31	
1) By Court	13	
2) By Jury	16	
3) Unknown	2	
II. Total Convicted of Lesser Offenses		21
A. Carrying a Concealed Weapon	7	
a) Pleaded Guilty	3	
b) Found Guilty	4	
1) By Court	2	
2) By Jury	2	
B. Assault and Battery and Carrying a Concealed Weapon	1	
a) Pleaded Guilty	1	
C. Assault and Battery	12	
a) Pleaded Guilty	6	
b) Found Guilty	6	
1) By Court	4	
2) By Jury	2	
D. Pointing and Discharging Firearm	1	
a) Pleaded Guilty	1	
III. Not Guilty		62
1) By Court	30	
2) By Jury	32	
IV. Nolle Prosequi		1
V. "No Bill" by Grand Jury		36
VI. Discharged upon Preliminary Examination		15
Total		185

---

[54]Black v. State, 103 Ohio St. 434, 133 N.E. 795 (1921); State v. Schaeffer, 96 Ohio St. 215, 117 N.E. 220 (1917). Also see Lattin, *Homicide,* 21 OHIO JURISPRUDENCE sections 22 *et seq.* (1932).

HOMICIDE IN AN URBAN COMMUNITY

tional killing by means of poison, or while perpetrating or attempting to perpetrate rape, arson, robbery, or burglary. Manslaughter differs from second degree murder in that malice is essential in murder in the second degree.[55]

Number Charged with Manslaughter in the First Degree

One hundred eighty-five persons, or 40.7 percent of all defendants charged with felonious homicides, were charged with manslaughter in the first degree.

Disposition Other Than by Trial or Upon a Plea of Guilty

Of these 185 persons: 15 were discharged upon preliminary examination by the municipal court; a *nolle prosequi* was entered by the county prosecutor in one case; and in 36 cases the grand jury refused to indict and returned "no bills."

The one case in which disposition was by *nolle prosequi*,[56] and the 15 in which the defendants were discharged upon preliminary examination are the only cases within these categories in the entire survey. That is, no cases in which the defendants were charged with either first or second degree murder were *"nolled"* or discharged upon preliminary examination. Also, of 41 cases in which the accused was charged with either first or second degree murder or with first degree manslaughter, and which cases were "no billed," 36 were cases in which the defendants were charged with first degree manslaughter. A partial explanation for the propensity of first degree manslaughter cases to fall within these categories is that, in many instances, the line of demarcation between first degree manslaughter and a lawful killing in self defense is exceedingly fine.

Conviction as a Result of Trial or Upon a Plea of Guilty

One hundred thirty-three persons were either convicted of manslaughter in the first degree as indicted, convicted of a lesser offense, or were found not guilty and released.

---

[55]Lattin, *Homicide,* 21 OHIO JURISPRUDENCE section 22 (1932).

[56]A *nolle prosequi* was entered in one other case. In this case, however, the defendant was immediately re-indicted for first degree murder, convicted, and electrocuted. Since the final disposition of the case was other than by *nolle prosequi,* for the purposes of the survey, it is excluded from the category of *"nolled"* cases.

HOMICIDE IN AN URBAN COMMUNITY

Number Found Not Guilty: Of the total number of persons charged with first degree manslaughter, 103 were indicted, pleaded not guilty, and had their guilt or innocence established by the deliberations of a court or a jury.[57] Sixty-two of these defendants, or 60.2 percent, were found not guilty without qualification and released.

Number Convicted: Seventy-one persons indicted for first degree manslaughter were either convicted of that offense or were convicted of a lesser offense. Fifty, or 70.4 percent, were convicted of first degree manslaughter; 12, or 16.9 percent, were convicted of assault and battery;[58] seven, or 9.9 percent, of carrying concealed weapons;[59] one defendant pleaded guilty to both assault and battery and carrying a concealed weapon; while one other was convicted of pointing and discharging a firearm.[60]

Number Pleading Guilty

Nineteen, or 38 percent, of the 50 defendants convicted of manslaughter in the first degree pleaded guilty. Fifty percent, or 6 out of 12, of the persons convicted of assault and battery pleaded guilty; three of the seven convicted of carrying concealed weapons did likewise, as did the one defendant convicted of both assault and battery and carrying a concealed weapon, and the one convicted of pointing and discharging a firearm.

Thus, while a total of 71 defendants indicted for first degree

---

[57]This classification excludes the 30 cases in which the defendants pleaded guilty.

[58]The penalty for assault and battery is a fine of not more than two hundred dollars or imprisonment for not more than six months, or both. Ohio Revised Code section 2901.25.

[59]The penalty upon conviction for the carrying of a concealed weapon is a fine of not more than five hundred dollars, or imprisonment in the county jail or workhouse not less than thirty days nor more than six months, or imprisonment in the penitentiary not less than one nor more than three years. Ohio Revised Code section 2923.01.

[60]Ohio Revised Code section 3773.04 provides: "No person shall, intentionally and without malice, point or aim a firearm at or toward another or discharge a firearm so pointed or aimed, or maim or injure a person by the discharge of a firearm so pointed or aimed. This section does not extend to cases in which firearms are used in self-defense, in the discharge of official duty, or in justifiable homicide." And section 3773.99 provides that: "Whoever violates section 3773.04 of the Revised Code shall be fined not less than one hundred dollars or imprisoned not more than one year, or both."

HOMICIDE IN AN URBAN COMMUNITY 39

manslaughter were convicted of some criminal offense, 40, or 56.3 percent, pleaded guilty to the offenses with which they were ultimately convicted.

Summary of Conviction Statistics

In summary, of the 133 defendants convicted as indicted, convicted of a lesser offense, or found not guilty and released: 37.6 percent were convicted of first degree manslaughter; 15.8 percent were convicted of various lesser offenses; and 46.6 percent were found not guilty of any offense.

Therefore, 53.4 percent of the above 133 defendants were convicted either of first degree manslaughter or of various lesser offenses. Since, however, 30 of these 133 defendants pleaded guilty to the offenses with which they were convicted, if this number is subtracted from the total 133, the over-all conviction rate drops from 53.4 percent to 39.8 percent.

Disposition and Method of Trial—Court or Jury

Although 185 persons were formally charged with first degree manslaughter, only 103 actually stood trial and were either convicted or found not guilty by the deliberations of a court or jury. Forty-nine of these 103 elected to be tried by a court; 52 chose trial by jury; and in two cases the method of trial is not known.

Of those tried by a court: 13, or 26.5 percent, were convicted as indicted of first degree manslaughter; six, or 12.2 percent, were convicted of lesser offenses; and 30, or 61.2 percent, were found not guilty.

The cases of the 52 defendants choosing trial by jury were disposed of as follows: 16, or 30.8 percent, were convicted of manslaughter; four, or 7.7 percent, were convicted of lesser offenses; and 32, or 61.5 percent, were found not guilty.

Probation

Eleven defendants convicted of manslaughter in the first degree received suspended sentences, and were placed upon probation for terms running from two years (in seven cases) to a maximum of five years. One defendant convicted of first degree manslaughter was given a suspended sentence and placed on probation for three years, and, in addition to the condition of good behavior,

TABLE 14

MANSLAUGHTER FIRST DEGREE—DISPOSITION OF CASES WHEN TRIED BY COURT OR BY JURY

I. Convicted of First Degree Manslaughter
    (a) Trial by court 26.5%
    (b) Trial by jury 30.8%

II. Convicted of Lesser Offenses
    (a) Trial by court 12.2%
    (b) Trial by jury 7.7%

III. Found Not Guilty
    (a) Trial by court 61.2%
    (b) Trial by jury 61.5%

was required to pay the victim's funeral expenses.[61] Also placed on probation was one convict found guilty of assault and battery and two convicted of carrying concealed weapons.

Thus, of 71 persons who were convicted of some criminal offense, and who were eligible for probation, only 14, or 19.7 percent, were placed upon probation.

TABLE 15

DEFENDANTS INDICTED FOR FIRST DEGREE MANSLAUGHTER— NUMBER OF SUSPENDED SENTENCES AND DURATION OF PROBATION

I. First Degree Manslaughter—Number Suspended Sentences 11
    1. Duration of Probation two years 7
        a. 6 pleaded guilty; 1 found guilty.
    2. Duration of probation three years 3
        a. 2 found guilty; 1 pleaded guilty.
    3. Duration of probation five years 1
        a. Defendant found guilty.

II. Carrying Concealed Weapon—Number Suspended Sentences 2
    1. Duration of probation one year 1
        a. Defendant found guilty.
    2. Duration of probation three years 1
        a. Defendant pleaded guilty.

III. Assault and Battery—Number Suspended Sentences 1
    1. Duration of probation six months 1
        a. Defendant found guilty.

---

[61] The defendant convicted of first degree manslaughter, who was placed on probation for five years, was first required to spend six months in the county jail. See Table 15.

Chapter III

RACES OF PERSONS ACCUSED OF FELONIOUS HOMICIDES

During the period of 1947-1953, of 462 persons formally charged with the commission of felonious homicides in Cuyahoga County, Ohio, 353, or 76.4 percent, were members of the Negro race. The remainder were members of the white race.[62]

A breakdown of the cases according to the specific homicides with which the defendants were charged in the first instance shows

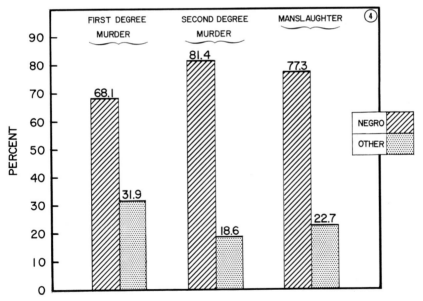

Graph 4. Races of Persons Accused of Committing Felonious Homicides.

---

[62]According to the United States Census, 1950, out of a total population in Cuyahoga County, Ohio, of 1,389,532 persons, 151,187, or 10.7 percent, were Negroes. In the City of Cleveland, out of total population of 914,808 persons, 147,847, or 16.2 percent, were Negroes.

that members of the Negro race accounted for: 68.1 percent of all defendants charged with first degree murder; 81.4 percent of those charged with second degree murder; and 77.3 percent of all charged with manslaughter in the first degree.

A. A COMPARISON OF RACE CONVICTION STATISTICS

1. Murder in the First Degree

A total of 92 Negro and white defendants indicted for first degree murder were either convicted as indicted, convicted of a lesser offense, or were found not guilty and released.[63] Twenty-

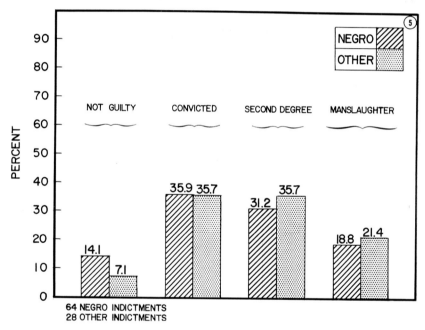

Graph 5. Comparison of Race Conviction Statistics—Murder in the First Degree. Total 92 Indictments.

---

[63] The first degree murder cases may be separated into those in which the defendants were charged only with the one count of deliberate and premeditated murder, and those in which they were charged, in addition, with one or more of the various felony murders, such as killing a police officer, killing by means of poison, or killing in perpetrating or attempting to perpetrate arson, rape, robbery, or burglary. Within the first category—deliberate and premeditated murder only—70.7 percent of the defendants were Negroes. In the second category, 67.4 percent were Negroes.

HOMICIDE IN AN URBAN COMMUNITY

TABLE 16

RACES OF DEFENDANTS—MURDER FIRST DEGREE

	White	Negro	Total
Total Charged with First Degree Murder	37	79	116
Convicted of First Degree Murder	10	23	33
Pleaded Guilty	0	4	4
Found Guilty	10	19	29
By Court	6	6	12
By Jury	4	13	17
Mercy Recommended	7	17	24
By Court	6	7	13
By Jury	1	10	11
Death	3	6	9
By Court	0	3	3
By Jury	3	3	6
Convicted of Lesser Offenses	16	32	48
Murder Second Degree	10	20	30
Pleaded Guilty	4	6	10
Found Guilty	6	14	20
By Court	2	7	9
By Jury	4	7	11
Manslaughter First Degree	6	12	18
Pleaded Guilty	5	3	8
Found Guilty	1	9	10
By Court	0	2	2
By Jury	1	7	8
Not Guilty	2	9	11
By Court	0	1	1
By Jury	2	8	10
Insane at Time of Trial	5	7	12
"No Bill" by Grand Jury	1	3	4
Abated by Death of Accused	2	0	2
Accused Not Apprehended	0	3	3
Trial of Case Pending	0	1	1
Disposition of Case Unknown	1	1	2

eight, or 30.4 percent, of the defendants within this classification were white. Sixty-four, or 69.6 percent, were Negroes.

Of the above 64 Negro defendants indicted for murder in the first degree: 35.9 percent were convicted as indicted; 31.2 percent were convicted of second degree murder; 18.8 percent of manslaughter in the first degree; and 14.1 percent were found not guilty.

In comparison: 35.7 percent of the 28 white defendants indicted for first degree murder were convicted of that offense; 35.7 percent were also convicted of murder in the second degree; 21.4 percent of first degree manslaughter; and only 7.1 percent were found not guilty and released.

Disposition and Method of Trial—Court or Jury: Of the total number of defendants indicted for murder in the first degree who stood trial, and who were found guilty or innocent as a result of the deliberations of a court or a jury, 42.1 percent of the white defendants chose trial by a court, as did 31.4 percent of the Negro defendants.

Seventy-five percent of the white defendants choosing trial by court were found guilty of murder in the first degree. The remainder were found guilty of murder in the second degree. Of the Negro defendants electing trial by court: only 37.5 percent were found guilty of first degree murder; 43.8 percent were convicted of second degree murder; 12.5 percent of first degree manslaughter; and 6.2 percent were found not guilty and released.

Of the almost 58 percent of the white defendants indicted for first degree murder who chose to be tried by a jury: 36.4 percent were convicted of murder in the first degree; 36.4 of second degree murder; 9.1 were found guilty of first degree manslaughter; and 18.2 percent were found not guilty of any offense and released. Disposition of the cases of the Negro defendants was as follows: 37.1 percent were found guilty of first degree murder; 20 percent of murder in the second degree; 20 percent of manslaughter; and 22.9 percent were found not guilty and discharged.

Recommendation of Mercy—by Court or Jury: Recommendations of mercy were made in 70 percent of the cases in which white persons were convicted of murder in the first degree. In the six cases in which white defendants were convicted by courts, the courts granted mercy. Where trial by jury was the means selected by four white defendants, mercy was recommended in only one instance.

Recommendations of mercy were made in 73.9 percent of all cases in which Negro defendants were convicted of first degree murder. In seven of ten cases in which the authority to grant mercy

HOMICIDE IN AN URBAN COMMUNITY

rested with the court upon conviction, mercy was extended. And in ten of 13 cases, or 76.9 percent, in which Negroes were convicted by a jury, mercy was recommended.

Probation: Since probation was not granted to any of the convicts eligible for probation, comparison on the basis of race is not possible.[64]

TABLE 17

RACES OF DEFENDANTS—MURDER SECOND DEGREE

	White	Negro	Total
Total Charged with Murder Second Degree	30	131	161
Convicted of Murder Second Degree	1	15	16
Pleaded Guilty	0	1	1
Found Guilty	1	14	15
By Court	1	3	4
By Jury	0	11	11
Convicted of Lesser Offenses	20	82	102
A. Manslaughter First Degree	20	80	100
Pleaded Guilty	14	43	57
Found Guilty	6	37	43
By Court	2	8	10
By Jury	4	29	33
B. Carrying a Concealed Weapon	0	1	1
Found Guilty	0	1	1
By Court	0	1	1
C. Assault and Battery	0	1	1
Pleaded Guilty	0	1	1
Not Guilty	5	28	33
By Court	2	10	12
By Jury	3	18	21
Not Guilty by Reason of Insanity	1	0	1
Insane at Time of Trial	3	1	4
"No Bill" by Grand Jury	0	1	1
Accused not Apprehended	0	2	2
Case Pending	0	1	1
Disposition of Case Unknown	0	1	1

---

[64]No person convicted of murder is eligible for probation. Ohio Revised Code section 2951.04.

2. Murder in the Second Degree

One hundred fifty-two persons indicted for second degree murder were either convicted of that offense, convicted of a lesser offense, or were found not guilty.[65]

Twenty-seven, or 17.8 percent, of these 152 defendants were white. One hundred twenty-five, or the remainder, were Negroes.

Of the 125 Negroes: 15, or 12 percent, were convicted as indicted of second degree murder; 80, or 64 percent, were convicted of first degree manslaughter; one defendant was convicted of carrying a concealed weapon; one of assault and battery; and 28, or 22.4 percent, were found not guilty without qualification and released.

In comparison, one, or 3.7 percent, of the 27 white defendants indicted for second degree murder was convicted of that offense. Twenty, or 74.1 percent, were convicted of first degree manslaughter; and five, or 18.5 percent, were found not guilty without qualification; and one was found not guilty by reason of insanity at the time of the commission of the offense.

Disposition and Method of Trial—Court or Jury: Excluding the one case in which a white defendant was found not guilty by reason of insanity at the time of the commission of the homicide,[66] of the defendants indicted for second degree murder who stood trial, and who were found guilty or innocent as a result of the deliberations of a court or a jury,[67] five out of 12, or 41.7 percent, of the white defendants elected to be tried by a court. The remainder chose trial by a jury. Only 27.5 percent, or 22 out of 80, of the Negro defendants within this category chose trial by court instead of trial by jury.

One, or 20 percent, of the five white defendants electing trial by court was found guilty of second degree murder; 40 percent were convicted of first degree manslaughter; and 40 percent were found not guilty without qualification and released.

Of the Negro defendants electing trial by a court: 13.6 percent

---

[65]Nine more persons were formally charged with second degree murder, but their cases were disposed of in ways not within this classification.

[66]This defendant elected trial by a court.

[67]This classification excludes cases in which the defendants pleaded guilty.

were convicted of second degree murder; 36.4 percent of first degree manslaughter; 4.5 percent of carrying a concealed weapon; and 45.5 percent were found not guilty without qualification and discharged.

None of the seven white persons electing trial by a jury was found guilty of second degree murder. However, 57.1 percent were convicted of first degree manslaughter and 42.9 percent were found not guilty without qualification and released.

Disposition of the cases of the 58 Negro defendants who chose trial by a jury was as follows: 19 percent were found guilty of second degree murder; 50 percent were convicted of first degree manslaughter; and 31 percent were found not guilty without qualification and discharged.

Probation: Of the 102 persons who were convicted of offenses other than second degree murder and who, therefore, were eligible for probation,[68] 20 were white persons and 82 were Negroes.

Only one white defendant convicted of first degree manslaughter was given a suspended sentence and placed on probation. Eighteen, or 22 percent, of the Negro convicts received suspended sentences. Seventeen of them had been convicted of first degree manslaughter and one had pleaded guilty to assault and battery.

3. Manslaughter in the First Degree

One hundred thirty-three persons indicted for manslaughter in the first degree were either convicted of that offense, convicted of a lesser offense, or were found not guilty without qualification.

Thirty-one, or 23.3 percent, of these 133 persons were white. The remainder were Negroes.

Of the 31 white persons indicted for first degree manslaughter: 11, or 35.5 percent, were convicted of that offense; three, or 9.7 percent, were convicted of assault and battery; and 17, or 54.8 percent, were found not guilty.

In comparison, 39, or 38.2 percent, of the 102 Negro defendants indicted for manslaughter in the first degree were convicted as indicted. Nine, or 8.8 percent, were convicted of assault and battery; seven, or 6.9 percent, of carrying a concealed weapon; one,

---

[68]See *supra* note 64.

TABLE 18

RACES OF DEFENDANTS—MANSLAUGHTER FIRST DEGREE

	White	Negro	Total
Total Charged with Manslaughter First Degree	42	143	185
Convicted of Manslaughter First Degree	11	39	50
Pleaded Guilty	4	15	19
Found Guilty	7	24	31
By Court	2	11	13
By Jury	4	12	16
Method of Trial Unknown	1	1	2
Convicted of Lesser Offenses	3	18	21
A. Assault and Battery	3	9	12
Pleaded Guilty	2	4	6
Found Guilty	1	5	6
By Court	0	4	4
By Jury	1	1	2
B. Carrying a Concealed Weapon	0	7	7
Pleaded Guilty	0	3	3
Found Guilty	0	4	4
By Court	0	2	2
By Jury	0	2	2
C. Assault and Battery and Carrying a Concealed Weapon	0	1	1
Pleaded Guilty	0	1	1
D. Pointing and Discharging Firearm	0	1	1
Pleaded Guilty	0	1	1
Not Guilty	17	45	62
By Court	8	22	30
By Jury	9	23	32
Nolle Prosequi	1	0	1
Discharged Upon Preliminary Examination	2	13	15
"No Bill" by Grand Jury	8	28	36

or approximately 1 percent, of both assault and battery and carrying a concealed weapon; one of the offense of pointing and discharging a firearm; and 45, or 44.1 percent, were found not guilty and released.

Disposition and Method of Trial—Court or Jury: Excluding the cases of one white and one Negro defendant in which the

HOMICIDE IN AN URBAN COMMUNITY

method of trial is unknown, of the number indicted for first degree manslaughter who actually stood trial, and who were found guilty or innocent as a result of the deliberations of a court or a jury,[69] 11 out of 24, or 45.8 percent, of the white defendants chose to be tried by a court rather than a jury. Thirty nine out of 77, or 50.6 percent, of the Negro defendants chose trial by a court rather than trial by jury.

Of the white persons choosing trial by court, 18.2 percent were found guity of manslaughter in the first degree. The rest were found not guilty.

In the cases of the Negro defendants electing a court trial: 28.2 percent were convicted as indicted of first degree manslaughter; 10.2 percent were found guilty of assault and battery; 5.1 percent of carrying a concealed weapon; and 56.4 percent were found not guilty and released.

Four of the 13 white defendants electing trial by a jury, or 30.8 percent, were convicted of first degree manslaughter. One, or 7.7 percent, was found guilty of assault and battery. Eight, or 61.5 percent, were found not guilty.

Disposition of the cases of the 38 Negro defendants choosing trial by jury was as follows: 12, or 31.6 percent, were found guilty as charged; one, or 2.6, was convicted of assault and battery; two, or 5.3 percent, were found guilty of carrying a concealed weapon; and 23, or 60.5 percent, were found not guilty and released.

Probation: Out of a total of 71 white and Negro defendants convicted of manslaughter in the first degree, or of some lesser offense, 14 were white and 57 were members of the Negro race. Five white defendants (35.7 percent) were given suspended sentences and placed on probation. All five of these had been convicted of first degree manslaughter.

Nine, or 15.8 percent, of the Negro convicts received suspended sentences and were placed on probation. Six of these had been convicted of manslaughter in the first degree, one of assault and battery, and two of carrying a concealed weapon.

---

[69]This classification excludes cases in which the defendants pleaded guilty.

TABLE 19

NEGROES ACCUSED OF KILLING WHITE PERSONS—FELONIOUS HOMICIDES

A. Total Charged with Murder First Degree ... 27
    I. Total Convicted Murder First Degree ... 15
        a) Pleaded Guilty ... 0
        b) Found Guilty ... 15
            1) By Court ... *5*
            2) By Jury ... *10*
        c) Mercy Recommended ... 9
            1) By Court ... *3*
            2) By Jury ... *6*
        d) Death ... 6
            1) By Court ... *2*
            2) By Jury ... *4*
    II. Total Convicted of Murder Second Degree ... 3
        a) Pleaded Guilty ... 2
        b) Found Guilty ... 1
            1) By Jury ... *1*
    III. Total Convicted of Manslaughter First ... 2
        a) Pleaded Guilty ... 1
        b) Found Guilty ... 1
            1) By Jury ... *1*
    IV. Not Guilty ... 3
            1) By Jury ... 3
    V. "No Bill" by Grand Jury ... 3
    VI. Case Pending ... 1

B. Total Charged with Murder Second Degree ... 3
    I. Total Convicted of Murder Second Degree ... 0
    II. Total Convicted of Manslaughter First Degree ... 1
        a) Pleaded Guilty ... 1
    III. Not Guilty ... 1
            1) By Jury ... 1
    IV. Defendant Not Apprehended ... 1

C. Total Charged with Manslaughter First Degree ... 3
    I. Total Convicted of Manslaughter First Degree ... 0
    II. Total Convicted of Assault and Battery ... 1
        a) Pleaded Guilty ... 1
    III. "No Bill" by Grand Jury ... 2

HOMICIDE IN AN URBAN COMMUNITY

B. NEGRO PERSONS ACCUSED OF KILLING WHITE PERSONS

A total of 353 Negro persons were formally charged with having committed felonious homicides during the period of the survey. Of this number, only 33, or 9.3 percent, were accused of killing white persons.

Fifteen, or 45.5 percent, of the Negro defendants accused of killing white persons were convicted of the offenses with which they were originally charged. Seven, or 21.2 percent, were convicted of lesser offenses; and four, or 12.1 percent, were found not guilty without qualification and released. In addition, five cases, or 15.2 percent, were "no billed;" one defendant has not been apprehended; and the case of one other is still pending.

As shown by Table 19, 27 of these 33 Negro defendants were charged with first degree murder. Fifteen were convicted of that offense. Only three were charged with second degree murder, and only three were charged with first degree manslaughter. None of these six was convicted of the offense with which he was charged.

C. WHITE PERSONS ACCUSED OF KILLING NEGRO PERSONS

Six white persons out of a total of 109 white defendants formally charged with felonious homicides, or 5.5 percent, were charged with killing Negroes.

As shown by Table 20, two were charged with first degree murder; two with second degree murder; and two with manslaughter in the first degree. None was convicted of the offense with which he was originally charged. Three, or 50 percent, were convicted of lesser offenses, and three were found not guilty without qualification and released.

D. A COMPARISON OF THE STATISTICS

As shown by Table 21, the most significant difference between the Negro-white statistics is in the percentage of whites convicted of the offenses with which they were originally charged as com-

TABLE 20

Whites Accused of Killing Negro Persons—Felonious Homicides

A. Total Charged with Murder First Degree 2
    I. Total Convicted of Murder First Degree 0
    II. Total Convicted of Murder Second Degree 1
        Found Guilty 1
          By Court 1
    III. Total Convicted of Manslaughter First Degree 1
        Pleaded Guilty 1

B. Total Charged with Murder Second Degree 2
    I. Total Convicted of Murder Second Degree 0
    II. Total Convicted of Manslaughter First Degree 1
        Found Guilty 1
          By Jury 1
    III. Not Guilty 1
        By Court 1

C. Total Charged with Manslaughter First Degree 2
    I. Total Convicted of Manslaughter First Degree 0
    II. Not Guilty 2
        By Jury 2

pared to the percentage of the Negroes so convicted. No white defendants were convicted as charged. However, 45.5 percent of the Negro defendants were convicted as charged. A plausible explanation which would account for a large part of this disparity may, perhaps, be found in the type of first degree murder charges placed against the Negro defendants accused of slaying white persons. Of the 27 Negroes charged with murder in the first degree, 20 were charged not only with a count of premeditated and deliberate murder in the first degree, but, in addition, were charged with one or more felony murder counts, such as killing a police officer, killing while perpetrating or attempting to perpetrate arson, robbery, burglary, or rape. Since only intent to kill need be proved in felony murders, in theory, a conviction should be easier to obtain than in cases in which, in addition to intent to kill, premeditation and deliberation have to be proved beyond a reasonable doubt.

HOMICIDE IN AN URBAN COMMUNITY

TABLE 21

PERSONS ACCUSED OF FELONIOUSLY SLAYING PERSONS OF ANOTHER RACE—COMPARISON OF CONVICTION STATISTICS

I.   Percentage Convicted as Charged
    a. Negroes accused of slaying whites 45.5%
    b. Whites accused of slaying Negroes 0.0%

II. Convicted of Lesser Offenses
    a. Negroes accused of slaying whites 21.2%
    b. Whites accused of slaying Negroes 50.0%

III. Not Guilty
    a. Negroes accused of slaying whites 12.1%
    b. Whites accused of slaying Negroes 50.0%

IV. Cases "No Billed"
    a. Negroes accused of slaying whites 15.2%
    b. Whites accused of slaying Negroes 0.0%

V.   Cases Pending
    a. Negroes accused of slaying whites 3.0%
    b. Whites accused of slaying Negroes 0.0%

VI. Accused Not Apprehended
    a. Negroes accused of slaying whites 3.0%
    b. Whites accused of slaying Negroes 0.0%

Fourteen of the Negro defendants who were tried on counts of premeditated and deliberate murder in the first degree, and also on one or more felony murder counts were convicted of murder in the first degree. In four of these 14 cases, they were found guilty of the felony murder counts, and were found not guilty of the counts of premeditated and deliberate murder. Unfortunately, in the other ten cases the records disclosed only that the defendants were convicted of first degree murder. They did not reveal whether the defendants were convicted of only one count or of more than one, and, if on only one count, whether it was for a felony murder or for deliberate and premeditated murder in the first degree.

Neither of the two white defendants charged with first degree murder was charged with a felony murder.

Of the seven Negro defendants charged only with premeditated and deliberate murder: only one was convicted as charged; two were convicted of second degree murder (one of whom pleaded

54   *HOMICIDE IN AN URBAN COMMUNITY*

guilty); two were found not guilty; one case was "no billed"; and one case is still pending. Of the two white defendants similarly charged: one was found guilty of second degree murder and the other pleaded guilty to first degree manslaughter.

Summary of Race Statistics

Number Convicted or Found Not Guilty: A total of 109 white persons were formally charged with the commission of felonious homicides during the seven years surveyed. Eighty-five white persons, or 78 percent, were either convicted as originally charged; convicted of a lesser offense; or were found not guilty without qualification and released.[70]

In comparison, of 353 Negro persons formally charged with felonious homicides: 291, or 82.4 percent, were convicted as charged; convicted of a lesser offense; or found not guilty without qualification and released.

Within the group of 85 white defendants and that of the 291 Negro defendants, the percentages of convictions as charged, convictions of lesser offenses, and findings of not guilty without qualification are, as shown by Table 22, almost identical.

TABLE 22

FELONIOUS HOMICIDES—COMPARISON OF CONVICTION STATISTICS
ACCORDING TO RACE AND DEFENDANTS

	White Defendants		*Negro Defendants*	
1.	Convicted as Charged	25.9%	Convicted as Charged	26.4%
2.	Convicted of Lesser Offense	45.9%	Convicted of Lesser Offense	45.4%
3.	Not Guilty	28.2%	Not Guilty	28.2%
	Total	100.0%		100.0%

Miscellaneous Disposition of Cases: In order to obtain a complete picture of the treatment accorded white and Negro persons accused of felonious homicides, the percentages of cases disposed

---

[70]This classification does not include the case of one white defendant found not guilty by reason of insanity at the time of the commission of the homicide.

of in ways other than by a conviction or by findings of not guilty without qualification must be considered.

Twenty-four white persons out of the total 109 formally charged with felonious homicides, or 22 percent, are within this category; as are 17.6 percent, or 62 out of the total 353 Negro defendants charged with felonious homicides. Table 23 shows the percentages and specific dispositions of these cases.

TABLE 23

MISCELLANEOUS DISPOSITION OF CASES

	White	Negro
I. Cases "No Billed"	8.3%	9.1%
II. Discharged Preliminary Hearing	1.8%	3.7%
III. Insane at Time of Trial	7.3%	2.3%
IV. Not Guilty by Reason of Insanity	0.9%	None
V. Nolle Prosequi	0.9%	None
VI. Accused Not Apprehended	None	1.4%
VII. Abated by Accused's Death	1.8%	None
VIII. Trial of Case Pending	None	0.6%
IX. Disposition of Case Unknown	0.9%	0.6%

While the greatest differences exist with respect to the percentages of Negroes and whites found insane at the time of trial, and in regard to those discharged upon preliminary examination, the actual number[71] of Negroes and whites within these categories seem too few to make the differences significant.

Recommendations of Mercy: Of all Negro and white defendants convicted of murder in the first degree, mercy was recommended in 70 percent of the cases involving white convicts, and in 73.9 percent of the cases involving Negroes.

---

[71]Eight whites out of 109 were found insane at the time of trial. Eight Negroes out of 353 were within this category.

Two whites out of 109 were discharged upon preliminary examination. Thirteen Negroes out of 353 were so discharged.

Probation: Fifteen percent of all eligible white convicts and 17.9 percent of all eligible Negro convicts received suspended sentences and were placed on probation.[72]

Conclusion: On the whole, there are no significant differences with respect to the disposition of the cases of white and Negro persons accused of felonious homicides. Certainly, there is no statistical evidence of racial discrimination.

---

[72]No person convicted of murder can be placed on probation. Ohio Revised Code section 2951.04.

Chapter IV

FEMALES ACCUSED OF FELONIOUS HOMICIDES

Of the total 462 persons of both sexes accused of felonious homicides during the period surveyed, 64, or 13.9 percent, were females. Fifty-two of these females were formally charged with slaying males. Twelve were accused of killing females.

A. FEMALES ACCUSED OF KILLING MALES

Murder in the First Degree

Only two of the 52 females accused of slaying males were charged with murder in the first degree.[73] One was found insane at the time of trial. The other was convicted of first degree murder, and, mercy having been recommended, was sentenced to life imprisonment.

Murder in the Second Degree

Twenty-two females were formally charged with second degree murder. One was convicted as charged; 14 were convicted of first degree manslaughter; one pleaded guilty to assault and battery; five were found not guilty without qualification; and one was found to be insane at the time of trial.

Manslaughter in the First Degree

Twenty-eight were charged with manslaughter in the first degree. Seven were convicted as charged; one pleaded guilty to assault and battery; and one was found guilty by a jury of assault and battery. Nine females were found not guilty without qualification; "no bills" were returned by the grand jury in eight cases;

---

[73]Both were charged with deliberate and premeditated murder. They were not charged with felony murders.

58   *HOMICIDE IN AN URBAN COMMUNITY*

and two females were discharged upon preliminary examination
of their cases.

TABLE 24

FEMALES ACCUSED OF FELONIOUSLY KILLING MALES

I. Number Charged with Murder First Degree 2
    A. Convicted of Murder First Degree *1*
        Found Guilty after Trial 1
            By Jury 1
        Mercy Recommended 1
            By Jury 1
    B. Insane at Time of Trial *1*

II Number Charged with Murder Second Degree 22
    A. Convicted of Murder Second Degree *1*
        Found Guilty After Trial 1
            By Jury 1
    B. Convicted of Manslaughter First Degree *14*
        Pleaded Guilty 5
        Found Guilty after Trial 9
            By Court 1
            By Jury 8
    C. Convicted of Assault and Battery *1*
        Pleaded Guilty 1
    D. Not Guilty *5*
        By Jury 5
    E. Insane at Time of Trial *1*

III. Charged with Manslaughter First Degree 28
    A. Convicted of Manslaughter First Degree 7
        Pleaded Guilty 2
        Found Guilty 5
            By Court 4
            By Jury 1
    B. Convicted of Assault and Battery 2
        Pleaded Guilty 1
        Found Guilty 1
            By Jury 1
    C. Not Guilty 9
        By Court 4
        By Jury 5
    D. "No Bill" 8
    E. Discharged upon Preliminary Examination 2

A Consideration of the Cases as a Whole

When all 52 of the "female killing male" cases are combined and considered as a whole, it is found that: 17.3 percent were convicted of the offenses with which they were originally charged; 32.7 percent were convicted of lesser offenses; 26.9 percent were found not guilty; "no bills" were returned in 15.4 percent; 3.8 percent were discharged upon preliminary examination; and the same percentage were found to be insane at the time of the trial of their cases.

Probation

One-third, or eight out of 24, of the female convicts eligible[74] received suspended sentences and were placed on probation.

Races of Female Defendants and Their Male Victims

Forty-three of the 52 females accused of killing males were Negroes. The remainder were white women. All the Negro women were accused of killing Negro men, and all the white females were accused of slaying white males.

Of the two females charged with first degree murder, one was white and one was Negro.[75]

Of the 22 women charged with second degree murder, 19 were Negroes and three were white women.

Five of the women accused of manslaughter in the first degree were white and 23 were Negroes.

The disposition of the cases of the Negro females charged with felonious homicides is as follows: 16.3 percent were convicted as charged; 30.2 were convicted of lesser offenses; 32.5 were found not guilty; 13.9 percent were "no billed"; 4.6 percent were discharged upon preliminary examination; and in one case, or 2.3 percent, the defendant was found insane at the time of trial.

Of the nine white female defendants accused of felonious homicides: two were convicted as originally charged;[76] four of

---

[74]No person convicted of murder can be placed on probation. Ohio Revised Code section 2951.04.

[75]The white defendant was found insane at the time of trial. The Negro defendant was convicted of first degree murder, mercy was recommended, and she was sentenced to life imprisonment.

[76]Both were originally charged with manslaughter in the first degree.

lesser offenses;[77] two cases were "no billed";[78] and in one the accused was found insane at the time of trial.[79].

Races of Female Convicts Placed on Probation: One white female out of a total of six who were eligible for probation,[80] or 16.7 percent, was placed on probation. Seven of 18 eligible Negro women, or 38.9 percent, were placed on probation.

The number of white female convicts involved is believed to be too small for the discrepancy in the probation statistics to be significant.

B. FEMALES ACCUSED OF KILLING FEMALES

Twelve females were formally charged with the felonious slaying of other females.

Murder in the First Degree

Only two of the 12 females were charged with murder in the first degree. One was found not guilty and the other was determined to be insane at the time of trial.

Murder in the Second Degree

Five females were charged with second degree murder. Three of them were convicted of the lesser offense of first degree manslaughter, and two were found not guilty of any offense and were released.

Manslaughter in the First Degree

Similarly, five women were accused of manslaughter in the first degree. Three were convicted of that offense and two were found not guilty.

A Consideration of the Cases as a Whole

When all the cases are combined and considered as a whole,

---

[77]Three of these four were charged with second degree murder and convicted of first degree manslaughter. The fourth was charged with first degree manslaughter and convicted of assault and battery.

[78]The defendants had been charged with first degree manslaughter.

[79]The defendant had been charged with first degree murder.

[80]No person convicted of murder can be placed on probation. Ohio Revised Code section 2951.04.

HOMICIDE IN AN URBAN COMMUNITY

of the 12 females charged with feloniously killing other females: 25 percent were convicted as charged; 25 percent were convicted of lesser offenses; 41.7 percent were found not guilty; and one woman, or 8.3 percent, was found to be insane at the time of trial.

TABLE 25

FEMALES ACCUSED OF FELONIOUSLY KILLING FEMALES

I. Charged with Murder First Degree	2
A. Not Guilty	1
By Jury	1
B. Insane at Time of Trial	1
II. Charged with Murder Second Degree	5
A. Convicted of Manslaughter First Degree	3
Pleaded Guilty	1
Found Guilty	2
By Court	1
By Jury	1
B. Not Guilty	2
By Court	1
By Jury	1
III. Charged with Manslaughter First Degree	5
A. Convicted of Manslaughter First Degree	3
Found Guilty	3
By Court	2
By Jury	1
B. Not Guilty	2
By Jury	2

Probation

Of six eligible[81] females convicted of slaying other females, four received suspended sentences and were placed on probation.

Races of Females Accused of Feloniously Slaying Females

Ten of the 12 females accused of feloniously killing other females were Negroes and two were white women. Both of the white defendants were accused of slaying white women. All the Negro defendants were charged with killing Negro women.

One of the two white defendants was indicted and tried for

---

[81]*Ibid.*

second degree murder. She was found guilty of first degree manslaughter. The other white defendant was indicted for first degree manslaughter, tried, and found guilty of that offense.

Of the ten Negro defendants: 20 percent were convicted as charged; 20 percent were convicted of lesser offenses; 50 percent were found not guilty; and one, or 10 percent, was found to be insane at the time of trial.

TABLE 26

FEMALE NEGRO DEFENDANTS ACCUSED OF FELONIOUSLY SLAYING FEMALES

I. Charged with Murder First Degree _____ 2
   A. Not Guilty _____ 1
       By Jury _____ 1
   B. Insane at Time of Trial_____ 1

II. Charged with Murder Second Degree_____ 4
   A. Convicted of Manslaughter First Degree_____ 2
       Pleaded Guilty_____ 1
       Found Guilty_____ 1
       By Court _____ 1
   B. Not Guilty _____ 2
       By Court _____ 1
       By Jury _____ 1

III. Charged with Manslaughter First Degree _____ 4
   A. Convicted of Manslaughter First Degree_____ 2
       Found Guilty_____ 2
       By Court _____ 1
       By Jury _____ 1
   B. Not Guilty _____ 2
       By Jury _____ 2

C. RACES OF FEMALE CONVICTS PLACED UPON PROBATION

Of the females convicted of killing females, two white convicts were eligible for probation[82] — one was placed upon probation. Three of the four Negro females eligible were placed upon probation.

When the statistics of both females convicted of slaying males

[82]*Ibid.*

and females convicted of slaying females are combined, it is found that of eight eligible white persons convicted, two, or 25 percent, received suspended sentences and were placed upon probation. In comparison, of 22 eligible Negro convicts within this combined category, ten, or 45.5 percent, were placed upon probation. Once again, however, it is believed that the total number of white convicts involved is too small to make the disparity significant.

D. FEMALE STATISTICS COMPARED WITH MALE STATISTICS

Conviction Statistics

Fifty-one females accused of felonious homicides were either convicted as charged; convicted of lesser offenses; or were found not guilty without qualification and were discharged. Within this classification: 23.5 percent of the females accused were convicted as originally charged; 39.2 percent were convicted of lesser offenses; and 37.2 percent were found not guilty.

In comparison, of 325 male defendants within such classification: 26.8 percent were convicted as originally charged; 46.5 percent were convicted of lesser offenses; and 26.8 were found not guilty without qualification and were discharged.

Probation Statistics

When the probation statistics of male and female convicts are compared, it is found that 40 percent of all eligible women convicts were given suspended sentences and placed upon probation. Only 13 percent of all eligible male convicts were placed upon probation.

Thus, before conviction the sex of the accused appears to have made little or no difference. After conviction, however, the figures indicate that sex is a significant factor in the granting of suspended sentences and probation.

Chapter V

MALES ACCUSED OF FELONIOUSLY SLAYING FEMALES

A total of 398 males were accused of felonious homicides during the period of 1947-1953. Ninety-eight of these males, or 24.6 percent, were charged with slaying women.

TABLE 27

MALES CHARGED WITH KILLING FEMALES

I. Total Charged with Murder First Degree— with Count of Arson, Rape, Robbery or Poison	9
A. Total Convicted as Charged	4
Pleaded Guilty	1
Found Guilty	3
By Court	0
By Jury	3
Mercy Recommended	1
By Jury	1
Death	3
By Court	1
By Jury	2
B. Convicted of Murder Second Degree	2
Pleaded Guilty	1
Found Guilty	1
By Jury	1
C. Convicted of Manslaughter First Degree	1
Found Guilty	1
By Jury	1
D. Not Guilty	1
By Jury	1
E. "No Bill" by Grand Jury	1
II. Total Charged with Deliberate and Premeditated Murder First Degree	30
A. Total Convicted as Charged	6
Found Guilty	6
By Court	2
By Jury	4
Mercy Recommended	5

HOMICIDE IN AN URBAN COMMUNITY

TABLE 27—*Continued*

By Court	2
By Jury	3
Death	1
By Jury	1
B. Convicted of Murder Second Degree	*14*
Pleaded Guilty	7
Found Guilty	7
By Court	6
By Jury	1
C. Convicted of First Degree Manslaughter	*4*
Pleaded Guilty	3
Found Guilty	1
By Jury	1
D. Not Guilty	*0*
E. Insane at Time of Trial	*5*
F. Not Apprehended	*1*
III. Total Charged with Murder in the Second Degree	*37*
A. Convicted as Charged	7
Found Guilty	7
By Court	2
By Jury	5
B. Convicted of First Degree Manslaughter	*24*
Pleaded Guilty	14
Found Guilty	10
By Court	4
By Jury	6
C. Not Guilty	*5*
By Court	1
By Jury	4
D. Insane at Time of Trial	*1*
IV. Charged with First Degree Manslaughter	*22*
A. Convicted as Charged	*11*
Pleaded Guilty	5
Found Guilty	6
By Court	4
Unknown	2
B. Convicted of Carrying a Concealed Weapon	2
Pleaded Guilty	1
Found Guilty	1
By Jury	1
C. Not Guilty	*5*
By Court	2
By Jury	3
D. "No Bill" by Grand Jury	*3*
E. Discharged upon Preliminary Examination	*1*

66 *HOMICIDE IN AN URBAN COMMUNITY*

MURDER IN THE FIRST DEGREE

Felony Murders

Nine of the 98 defendants were charged with felony murders, in addition to premeditated and deliberate murder in the first degree.

Of these nine: four were charged with intentional killings while perpetrating or attempting to perpetrate robbery and rape;[83] one with killing while perpetrating robbery;[84] one while perpetrating rape;[85] one with purposely killing by means of poison;[86] one with killing while perpetrating or attempting to perpetrate robbery and with killing by means of poison;[87] and one with killing while perpetrating arson.[88]

Four, or 44.4 percent, of these nine defendants were convicted of first degree murder; 33.3 percent were convicted of lesser offenses; one was found not guilty; and one case was "no billed" by the grand jury.

Premeditated and Deliberate Murder

Thirty males were charged only with the one count of deliberate and premeditated murder in the first degree. Six of these were convicted as charged of first degree murder; 14 were convicted of second degree murder; four of first degree manslaughter; five were insane at the time of trial; and one has not been apprehended.

MURDER IN THE SECOND DEGREE

A total of 37 males were charged with second degree murder. Seven were found guilty as charged; 24 were convicted of first

---

[83]Two of these defendants were convicted of first degree murder and electrocuted. (It is not known whether they were convicted on all the counts of first degree murder with which they were charged.) One defendant pleaded guilty to second degree murder. The case of the fourth was "no billed."

[84]A jury found the defendant guilty on the felony murder count and also on the count of premeditated murder. Mercy was recommended.

[85]The defendant was convicted of second degree murder.

[86]The defendant pleaded guilty to both counts of first degree murder and was electrocuted.

[87]After jury trial, the defendant was found not guilty and released.

[88]Defendant was convicted, after trial, of first degree manslaughter.

degree manslaughter; five were found not guilty; and one was insane at the time of trial.

MANSLAUGHTER IN THE FIRST DEGREE

Twenty-two males accused of killing females were formally charged with first degree manslaughter. Eleven were convicted of that offense. Two defendants were convicted of the offense of carrying a concealed weapon; five were found not guilty; one was discharged upon preliminary examination; and three cases were "no billed."

A CONSIDERATION OF THE CASES AS A WHOLE

When all of the "male killing female" statistics are combined, it is found that of the 98 males charged with felonious homicides: 28.6 percent were convicted of the offenses with which they were originally charged; 47.9 percent were convicted of lesser offenses; 11.2 were found not guilty without qualification and released; 6.1 were determined to be insane at the time of trial; "no bills" were returned in 4.1 percent of the cases; one defendant was discharged upon preliminary examination; and one has not been apprehended.

Probation

Of 42 males eligible for probation after conviction of offenses against females, seven, or 16.7 percent, received suspended sentences and were placed upon probation.[89]

Races of Defendants and Victims—
Males Accused of Slaying Females

Of the 98 males charged with feloniously slaying females, 68 males were Negroes and 30 were white persons.

Sixty-five of the Negro males were charged with killing Negro females. Twenty-nine of the white males were accused of killing white females.

Thus, only three Negroes were charged with killing white women. These three Negro males were charged with the slaying

---

[89]See note 80 *supra.*

68 HOMICIDE IN AN URBAN COMMUNITY

of two white females while perpetrating, or attempting to perpetrate, rape and robbery. The grand jury returned a "no bill" in the case of one defendant; the second pleaded guilty to second degree murder; and the third was found guilty of first degree murder and sentenced to death.

The one white male accused of slaying a Negro female was indicted for deliberate and premeditated murder in the first degree. He pleaded guilty to manslaughter in the first degree.

Of 60 Negro males[90] who were either convicted of some offense or were found not guilty: 33.3 percent were convicted as originally charged; 53.3 percent were convicted of lesser offenses; and 13.3 percent were found not guilty. In comparison, of 26 white males[91] within this category: 30.8 percent were convicted as originally charged; 57.7 percent were convicted of lesser offenses; and 11.5 percent were found not guilty and discharged.

Races of Male Convicts Placed upon Probation

Of 28 Negro convicts eligible to be placed upon probation,[92] five, or 17.8 percent, were given suspended sentences and placed upon probation. In comparison, of 14 white male defendants convicted of offenses against females, and who were eligible for probation, two, or 14.3 percent received suspended sentences and were placed upon probation. One of these two white male convicts had been charged with murdering a Negro female, and had pleaded guilty to mansaughter in the first degree.

A COMPARISON OF MALE-KILLING-MALE STATISTICS WITH MALE-KILLING-FEMALE STATISTICS

Two hundred and thirty-nine males accused of feloniously slaying males were either convicted of some criminal offense or were found not guilty. Of this number: 24.7 percent were convicted

---

[90]The cases of the remaining eight Negro males accused of slaying females were disposed of as follows: three were "no billed"; three defendants were insane at time of trial; one case was discharged upon preliminary examination; and one accused has not been apprehended.

[91]The cases of the four remaining white males were disposed of in the following manner: three were insane at time of trial; and one case was "no billed."

[92]See note 80 *supra*.

HOMICIDE IN AN URBAN COMMUNITY

as originally charged; 43.5 percent were convicted of lesser offenses; and 31.8 percent were found not guilty.

Of 86 males accused of slaying females who were either convicted or found not guilty: 32.6 percent were convicted as charged; 54.6 were convicted of lesser offenses; and only 12.8 percent were found not guilty.

Probation

As previously set forth, 16.7 percent of all males convicted of offenses against females, and who were eligible to be placed upon probation,[93] received probation.

Only 11.8 percent of all males eligible for probation after conviction of offenses against males received probation, however.

---

[93]See note 80 *supra*.

Chapter VI

AGES OF PERSONS CHARGED WITH FELONIOUS HOMICIDES

The ages of 439 of the 462 defendants charged with felonious homicides are known. Graph 6 shows the ages in five-year age groups and the number and percent of defendants within each group.[94]

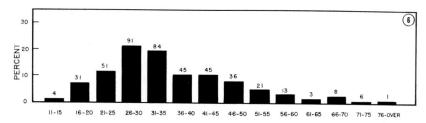

Graph 6. Ages of 439 Persons Charged with Felonious Homicide.

The defendants are relatively young. Seventy-two percent are within the ages of 21 through 45, and 87.2 percent are within the ages of 16 through 50.

For any single five-year age classification, the highest percentage is in the 26-30 group (20.7%); and the 31-35 age group (19.1%). As might be expected, the lowest percentages are in the 76-year and over group (0.2%); the 66-70 group (0.7%); and the 11-15 year classification (0.9%).

In summary, it appears that it is neither the very young nor the old who become involved in the criminal law to the extent of being formally charged with felonious homicide. It is the so-called "young adult." One can only speculate as to why this is so. Perhaps persons within this classification have more social contacts

---

[94]For the ages of decedents in justifiable homicides, see Graph 7 *infra*.

HOMICIDE IN AN URBAN COMMUNITY

than in older or younger classifications, and therefore increase the chances of the occurrence of personal violence. They may also engage more frequently in particular activities such as drinking and gambling—activities which are conducive to quarreling and violence. Another factor may be that one is easier to offend, and more aggressive when offended, at this stage of life than in another. One must, however, remember that neither age nor any other factor can be singled out and regarded as the sole cause of homicide. Rather, it is believed that homicide is the result of a multiplicity of factors which have interacted one upon the other. It " . . . is a resultant of all the forces impinging upon the individual plus the characteristics of his personality."[95]

---

[95]Elliot and Merrill, SOCIAL DISORGANIZATION 161 (1941).

Chapter VII

TYPES OF CONFLICTS CULMINATING IN FELONIOUS HOMICIDES

While the basic causes of felonious homicides lie too deep and are too complex to be gathered from police, court, and coroners' reports, the type situations out of which they arise, and the "triggering" or precipitating causes and motives are obtainable from such reports.

As was also found by Professor Henry A. Bullock, in his survey of homicide in Houston, Texas,[96] the three categories into which felonious homicides fell most frequently were: (1) quarrels of a mostly petty nature; (2) marital discords in which one spouse kills the other;[97] and (3) love or sex disputes in which the deceased is slain by one other than his spouse or "common law" mate.[98]

The following homicides illustrate the type cases within the first category:

(1) D was sitting on the bed in his room. V, D's friend of many years, entered the room and headed for the refrigerator. D said: "Where you going?" V replied: "I'm going to get me a beer out of your refrigerator." D retorted: "Nobody gets no beer out of my ice box unless I tells him to," whereupon V whirled, pulled out a knife, and said: "The hell with you and your ice

---

[96]See Henry Allen Bullock, *Urban Homicide in Theory and Fact,* 46 JOURNAL OF CRIMINAL LAW, CRIMINOLOGY, AND POLICE SCIENCE 572 (1955). Experimentation with many classifications found none that portrayed the Cuyahoga County cases as precisely as these three categories.

[97]Included within this category are cases in which a "common-law" spouse kills his or her mate. And the term "common-law" spouse is used here in both its lay and its legal sense. That is, it is used to denote persons who are merely living together on a permanent or semi-permanent basis but who are not legally married (lay sense); and also to denote informal marriages of the type which Ohio regards as valid and binding.

[98]These conclusions are based upon 350 cases in which the police reports, court records, and coroners' reports contained sufficient data for reasonably accurate judgments to be made.

The term "common law" mate is used here in both its lay and its legal sense.

Photograph 1. The social club of the lower economic group is often the scene of conflicts between friends.

box, too!" D reached under the mattress, pulled out a pistol, and shot V three times, killing him instantly. D admitted having had "a couple beers." Test of V's blood revealed he had been drinking, but was not intoxicated.

(2) D came home in his car and found a garbage truck blocking his driveway. He shouted at the garbage men to move the truck; cursed them and used insulting language. V and other garbage men argued with him and threw garbage at him. D got out of his car, went into his home, came out carrying a rifle, and fired at the men, killing V. There was evidence that D had been drinking "heavily." Blood alcohol test on V was negative.

(3) D and V argued about $3.00 which V claimed D owed him. Later the same afternoon, V walked unannounced into D's house. Whereupon D shot V. There was no evidence that D had been drinking and V's blood alcohol test was negative.

In marital discords in which one spouse killed the other, gen-

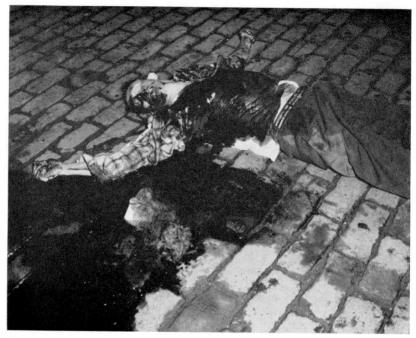

Photograph 2. A victim with 0.23% blood alcohol, 0.27% urine alcohol found on the street outside the social club pictured in photograph 1.

erally the subject of conflict was a relatively serious nature and had been a source of discord for some time. Characteristic cases within this category are the following:

(1) D was a chronic alcoholic with a history of delirium tremens. His excessive drinking had been the subject of previous conflict between D and his wife, V. On the day of the homicide, D had, according to his own testimony, "a few drinks." On arriving home, his wife looked at him and said: "Drunk, get out of here!" D walked into the next room, returned with a shotgun and killed V. V had not been drinking.

(2) D and V were a man and wife in their late sixties. V, the wife, was very friendly with a couple living next door, and spent a great deal of time in the neighbors' home. D believed V was having sexual relations with the male neighbor. His sole basis for belief was the fact V spent so much time next door. He also believed that V was planning to draw all the money out of their joint savings account and "run off with the neighbor." D,

Photograph 3. Arguments between spouses may begin in the kitchen where cutting weapons are handy.

a short time before the homicide, withdrew all the money in his and V's account and deposited it in a bank in a part of town where he was not known. V did not know D had withdrawn the money. On the night of the homicide, D, in the early hours of the morning, got out of bed to get a drink of water. V berated him for getting up. On the way back from the kitchen, D stumbled over a claw hammer. He took the hammer, returned to the bedroom, and beat his wife to death. Neither had been drinking.

(3) V, D's wife, told him she was leaving him. An argument ensued and D shot and killed V. D stated that V had been married and divorced once before and now was going to break up his marriage and he killed her "so she wouldn't break up any more marriages!" Neither had been drinking.

(4) D and her husband, V, argued about D's running around with other men. D said her husband hit her and that she was afraid he was going to beat her up, as he had done on previous

Photograph 4. The wife is slain in the kitchen with the scissors wielded by her husband.

occasions. (V denied hitting her this time, but admitted having hit her on previous occasions. A witness stated that V had swung at D.) D threw boiling lye in V's face. Since V lived several days, no test for alcohol was made. V, however, stated he had had "several bottles of beer." A witness stated that V "was feeling pretty good." V stated that D had been drinking, but was not intoxicated.

Cases illustrative of the third category are the following:

(1) During a drinking party at D's home, D and V argued over a girl with whom D was living. V wanted the girl to come live with him. V threatened D and reached into his pocket, whereupon D shot V several times, killing V instantly. No weapon was found in V's pockets. D admitted having had "a few drinks," but stated he was not intoxicated. V's blood alcohol test revealed that he was under the influence of alcohol.

(2) D, male, had lived with X, a female, for 3 years. V

Photograph 5. Homicides committed during robberies receive much publicity, but do not represent as great a number of killings as do marital discords and quarrels between friends.

moved in and began living with X. D broke into the house and struck V on the head with a baseball bat while V was asleep. Neither D nor V had been drinking.

(3) D, age 33, was a boy friend of V, a girl of 13, and was a roomer in the house in which V lived. D accused V of having other boy friends and of "giving him the run around." An argument ensued and D stabbed V. The victim had not been drinking. A witness stated that D had had one beer.

Chapter VIII

JUSTIFIABLE HOMICIDES

For the purposes of this survey, justifiable homicide is defined as the intentional killing of a human being, without evil design, and under such circumstances of necessity or duty as render the act proper.[99] A homicide is justifiable, and no penalty whatever is imposed, in the following situations:

1. When a person is necessarily killed, either by a peace officer or by a private person, in order to prevent him from committing a felony by violence or surprise.

2. When a person is necessarily killed in effecting an arrest for a felony committed by him, or in preventing his escape after he has been arrested and is in custody.

3. When a person who is feloniously assaulted, and who is himself without fault, kills his assailant to save himself from death or great bodily harm.

4. When a person becomes engaged in a sudden affray or combat, and in the course of the affray or combat necessarily kills his adversary to save himself from death or great bodily harm.[100]

---

[99]BLACK'S LAW DICTIONARY (3d ed. 1933). This definition includes all cases which would be classified as justifiable homicides at common law. For simplicity, it also includes one of the two types of homicides which at common law would have been classified as excusable homcides. The one it includes is *homicide se defendendo* (self defense upon a sudden affray), where one necessarily kills another, after becoming engaged in a sudden affray, in order to save himself from reasonably apparent danger of death or great bodily harm. Clark & Marshall, LAW OF CRIMES Sec. 273 (5th ed. 1952). It does not include the second type of excusable homicide at common law known as *homicide per infortunium*, where a person unfortunately kills another in doing a lawful act, without an intent to harm, and without criminal negligence. Clark & Marshall, LAW OF CRIMES 370 (5th ed.). Cases of this latter type are not included in this survey.

[100]Clark & Marshall, LAW OF CRIMES Secs. 267, 278 (5th ed. 1952). There are two other justifiable homicide situations, of which no cases are included in this survey. They are: (1) when a homicide is necessarily committed either by a private person or a peace officer in suppressing a riot; (2) when a person convicted of a capital offense and sentenced to death is executed by the proper officer. Clark & Marshall, LAW OF CRIMES Sec. 268 (5th ed. 1952). For an excellent discussion of Ohio Law, see Lattin, *Homicide*, 21 OHIO JURISPRUDENCE Secs. 34 *et seq.* (1932).

HOMICIDE IN AN URBAN COMMUNITY 79

NUMBER OF JUSTIFIABLE HOMICIDES

In Cuyahoga County, Ohio, from January 1, 1947 to December 31, 1953, 157 homicides were ruled justifiable by the various prosecutors within the county. These homicides may be divided into two categories: those involving private persons and those in which the decedents were killed by police officers.

CASES INVOLVING PRIVATE PERSONS

As shown by Table 28, in 122 cases the decedents were slain by private persons.

Ninety-seven, or 79.5 percent, of the persons slain were Negroes; and 25 were white persons. Eight Negroes were killed by white persons. In the cases of four Negro decedents, the races

TABLE 28

JUSTIFIABLE HOMICIDES—DECEDENTS KILLED BY PRIVATE PERSONS

I. Total number of cases			122
II. Color of deceased: White 25	Negro 97		
III. Sex of deceased: Male 117	Female 5		
IV. No. Negro killed by white: 8			
V. No. Negro killed by Negro: 85			
VI. No. Negro killed by color unknown: 4			
VII. No. Whites killed by white: 22			
VIII. No. Whites killed by Negro. 2			
IX. No. Whites killed by Unknown: 1			
X. No. Males killed by males: 82			
a. Color of deceased: White 21	Negro 61		
b. Color of defendant: White 26	Negro 52	Unknown 4	
XI. No. Males killed by females: 35			
a. Color of deceased: White 4	Negro 31		
b. Color of defendant: White 3	Negro 32		
XII. No. Females killed by males: 3			
a. Color of deceased: White 0	Negro 3		
b. Color of defendant: White 1	Negro 1	Unknown 1	
XIII. No. Females killed by females: 2			
a. Color of deceased: White 0	Negro 2		
b. Color of defendant: White 0	Negro 2		

of their slayers are not known. Only two white decedents were slain by Negro persons; and in only one instance was the race of a white decedent's killer unknown.

Of the total 122 decedents, 117, or approximately 96 percent, were males. And 82 of these 117 male decedents, or 70.1 percent, were slain by males. Thirty-five males were slain by females.

In the cases of the five women decedents, three were killed by males and two were slain by females.

TYPE HOMICIDE SITUATIONS

Approximately 85 percent of the justifiable homicide cases involving only private persons were cases of self-defense, and arose out of relatively trivial arguments of the type set forth in the section on felonious homicides. Of the remaining 15 percent of the cases, three-fourths involved robberies or attempted robberies, and one-fourth were cases in which the slayers intervened in the defense of other persons.

CASES INVOLVING POLICE OFFICERS

Thirty-five persons were slain by police officers in Cuyahoga County during the seven years surveyed. The homicides were ruled justifiable. All of the officers were males and all of the decedents were males.

TABLE 29

JUSTIFIABLE HOMICIDES—DECEDENTS KILLED BY POLICE OFFICERS

I.	Total number of cases	35
II.	Color of deceased: White 9 Negro 26	
III.	Sex of deceased: Male 35 Female 0	
IV.	No. Negroes killed by white officers:	18
V.	No. Negroes killed by Negro officers:	5
VI.	No. Negroes killed by white and Negro officers:	1
VII.	No. Whites killed by white officers:	9
VIII.	No. Whites killed by Negro officers:	0
IX.	No. Negroes killed by color unknown officers:	2
X.	No. Males killed by males:	35

Twenty-six of the decedents were Negroes. Nine were white. Five of the Negro decedents were killed by Negro officers; 18 by white officers; one was killed by both a white and a Negro officer; and in two instances the race of the officers is not known. All of the white decedents were slain by white officers.

In 34 of the cases, the decedents were either killed by the officers in an attempt to effect the arrest of the decedents, or in trying to prevent the decedents' escape after they had been arrested and were in the custody of the officers. In one case, the decedent entered the dining room of a hotel where his common law wife was working as a waitress. He apparently intended to kill her. Several police officers were there eating lunch. When decedent saw them, he began shooting at them. In an exchange of shots, he was killed.

AGES OF THE DECEDENTS

Of the 157 cases of justifiable homicide which occurred during the period surveyed, the ages of 155 of the decedents are known.

Graph 7 shows the ages in five-year groups and the number and percent of the 155 decedents within each age group. The decedents were relatively young: 80.6 percent were in the 16-45 age group; and 86.5 percent were in the 16-50 group.

For single five-year classifications, the highest percentages fall in the 36-40 age group (20.6%); the 26-30 group (19.4%); and the 31-35 group (15.5%). From age 56 and up, the number of decedents within each five-year group is very low. Only the 56-60 group with four cases, and the 66-70 with two cases, contains more than

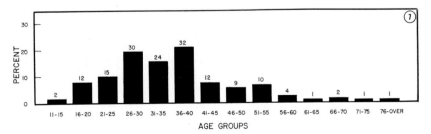

Graph 7. Ages of Decedents—155 Justifiable Homicides.

one case. Similarly, the 11-15 year-old group accounts for only two decedents.

Thus, as was found in regard to felonious homicides,[101] it was neither the very young nor the old who became involved in situations of this type, but the so-called "young adult."

---

[101]See Graph 6 *supra*.

Chapter IX

METHODS USED TO SLAY VICTIMS

A. HOMICIDES OTHER THAN JUSTIFIABLE HOMICIDES

From January 1, 1947 to December 31, 1953, 505 persons were the victims in either felonious homicides or in killings which, for the purposes of the survey, are listed as unclassified homicides (see Table 1).

As shown by Graph 8, the weapons and methods used were simple ones.[102] Firearms were employed in 55.2 percent of the deaths. Hand guns—pistols and revolvers—were used in 46.9 percent; shotguns in 6.9 percent; and rifles in 1.4 percent.

Cutting or piercing instruments, with a total of 26.7 percent, ranked second in frequency of use. Specifically, knives accounted for 21.2 percent of all deaths, and perhaps even more, for some knives were undoubtedly used in the 3.4 percent of deaths in which all that is known is that the victims were "stabbed."

Non-cutting and non-piercing—or blunt—instruments of many varieties, from baseball bats to bricks and floor lamps, ranked third in frequency of use (6.7 percent).

Manual assaults accounted for 6.1 percent of the cases.[103] Strangulation and asphyxiation for 3 percent. No other single category accounted for more than 0.6 percent of the deaths during the period surveyed.

Race Differences in Choice of Weapons

Firearms were, by far, the favorite weapons of both whites and

---

[102]These percentages are based upon a total of 505 weapons and methods employed to slay 505 victims. For example, if five victims were shot and killed by one assailant at the same time, firearms would be credited with accounting for five deaths. Conversely, if two assailants, using two guns, both shot and killed one victim, firearms would be credited with only one death.

[103]That is, assaults involving the use of hands, fists, feet, or other body-to-body contacts, except use of the hands in strangulation and asphyxiation.

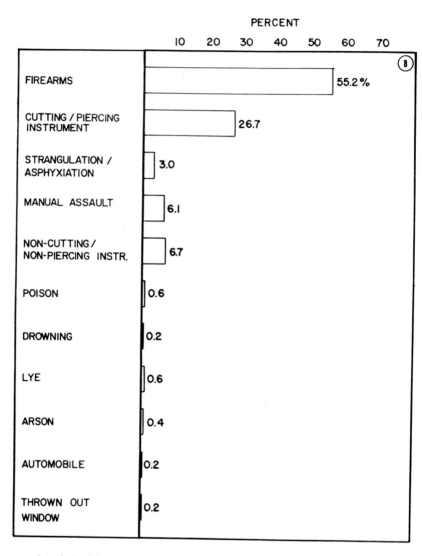

Graph 8. Weapons and Methods Used in 505 Homicides Other Than Justifiable Homicides.

Photograph 6. Firearms are the weapons used in over one-half the homicides.

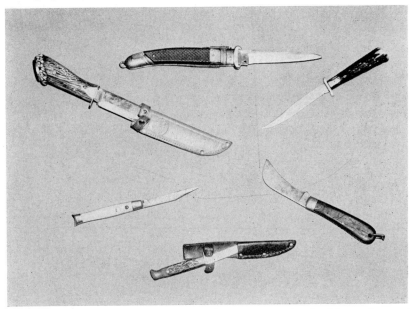

Photograph 7. One-quarter of the slayings are committed with cutting and piercing instruments.

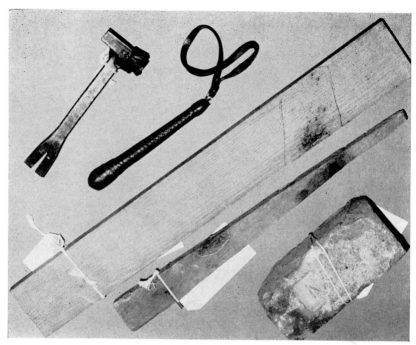

Photograph 8. Blunt instruments are used in nearly seven of every 100 homicides, the third ranking weapon of death.

Negroes. They were used by 51.3 percent of the alleged white slayers and 56.3 percent of the alleged Negro killers.[104]

While cutting and piercing instruments ranked as the second choice of both races, they were employed by 31.9 percent of the alleged Negro assailants,[105] but by only 12.8 percent of the white assailants.

---

[104]These percentages are based upon the weapons and methods used by 357 Negro assailants and 117 white assailants. The following method was used in compiling these totals: the slaying of one victim by two white assailants, both assailants having guns and having shot the victim, was counted as two deaths by firearms by white assailants. Conversely, where one white assailant shot and killed two victims contemporaneously, white assailants would be credited with having chosen firearms in one instance. The race of the slayers of 25 victims is unknown.

[105]One cutting instrument historically supposed to be popular with members of the Negro race is the straight razor. The statistics do not support this, for in only three instances did the records show the use of this weapon. Another weapon com-

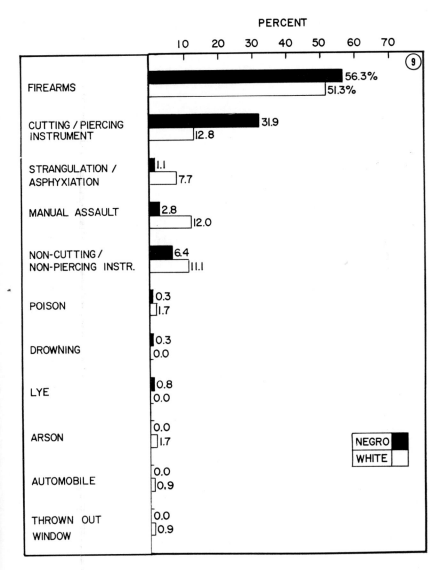

Graph 9. Weapons Used—Comparison by Race—474 Homicides Other Than Justifiable Homicides.

---

monly associated with Negro assailants is the so-called "switch-blade" knife. Unfortunately, the police and coroner's records did not, in most instances, identify the type knife used with such exactness. No conclusions can, therefore, be stated with respect to the use of this weapon.

88   *HOMICIDE IN AN URBAN COMMUNITY*

Non-cutting and non-piercing instruments were used more frequently by white assailants (11.1%) than by Negro assailants (6.4%). This was also true of strangulation: whites—7.7 percent; Negroes—1.1 percent; and of manual assault: whites—12 percent; Negroes—2.8 percent.

Sex Differences in Choice of Weapons

Cutting and piercing instruments were the favorite weapons of female assailants, with firearms the second type weapon most frequently used.[106] Thus, 50.8 percent of the women assailants used cutting and piercing instruments, as compared to 23.5 percent of the male assailants. Only 29.2 percent of the female assailants employed firearms, as compared to 59.2 percent of the males.

While strangulation and asphyxiation were employed by 6.2 percent of the female slayers, their victims were all infants. Similarly, the one victim thrown out an upstairs window was a newborn baby, and the victim drowned was a small child.

B. JUSTIFIABLE HOMICIDES

Homicides Committed by Private Persons

In the 122 cases of justifiable homicides in which the slayers were private persons and not police officers, firearms were used in 66.4 percent. Pistols and revolvers were employed in 59.8 percent of the 122 cases; rifles in 2.5 percent; and shotguns in 4.1 percent.

Again,[107] cutting and piercing instruments ranked second in frequency of use, accounting for 22.1 percent of the weapons used. Non-cutting and non-piercing instruments ranked third with a total of 6.6 percent; and manual assaults accounted for 4.9 percent of the 122 deaths.

Race Differences in Choice of Weapons by Private Persons

Firearms were also the weapons most frequently employed by both whites and Negroes in justifiable homicides committed by private persons. As shown by Graph 12, firearms were used by 63.2

---

[106]The methods of totaling the sex of the assailants are the same as those used in totaling the races of the assailants. See explanation in footnote 104 *supra*. The sex of the slayers of 25 victims is unknown.

[107]See Graph 8 *supra*.

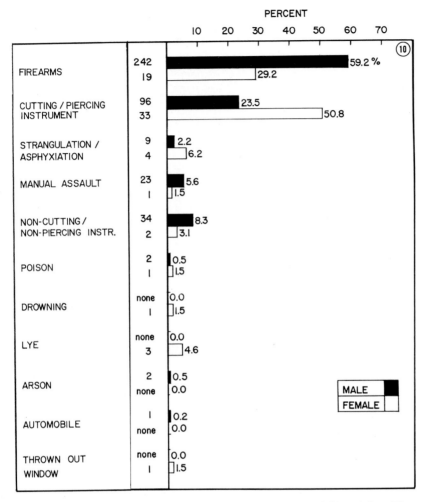

Graph 10. Weapons Used—Comparison by Sex—474 Homicides Other Than Justifiable Homicides.

percent of the 87 Negro slayers and 73.3 percent of the 30 white slayers. (The races of the slayers are not known in five of the total 122 cases in this category.)

Cutting and piercing instruments ranked as the second choice of the Negro slayers, and were employed by them in 27.6 percent of the cases. They were used by only 10 percent (three cases) of the white slayers, however.

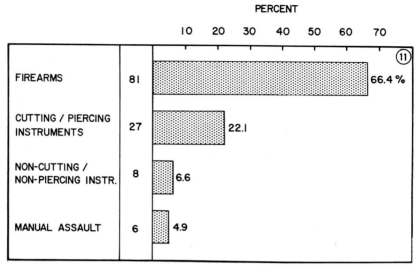

Graph 11. Weapons and Methods Used in 122 Justifiable Homicides.

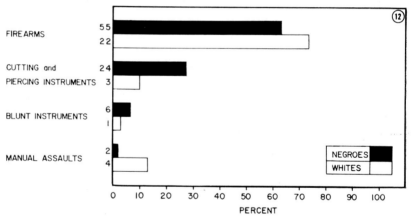

Graph 12. Weapons Used—Comparison by Race—117 Justifiable Homicides.

Manual assaults accounted for four, or 13.3 percent, of the white cases; but for two, or only 2.3 percent, of the Negro deaths.

Non-cutting and non-piercing instruments were used in six, or 6.9 percent, of the Negro deaths; but in only one, or 3.3 percent, of the white deaths.

Sex Differences in Choice of Weapons by Private Persons

Firearms also were the weapons most frequently used by both male and female slayers. They were employed by 67.1 percent of the males, and by 64.9 percent of the females.

Cutting and piercing instruments were used by 18.8 percent of the men, and by 29.7 percent of the female slayers in the justifiable homicides involving private persons.

Two female slayers, or 5.4 percent, used non-cutting and non-piercing instruments: a flat iron and a pop bottle; while six males, or 7.1 percent, used non-cutting and non-piercing instruments.

No deaths by manual assault occurred in the cases involving female slayers; and this method was used in only six, or 7.1 percent, of the male cases.

Homicides Committed by Police Officers

In the 35 cases of justifiable homicide in which the slayers were police officers, firearms were the weapons used in every instance.

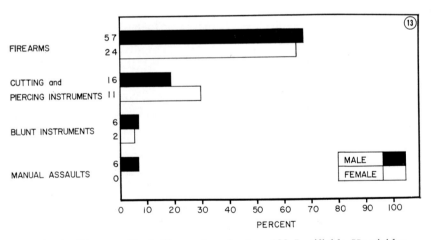

Graph 13. Weapons Used—Comparison by Sex—122 Justifiable Homicides.

Chapter X

ALCOHOL STATISTICS

A. FELONIOUS HOMICIDES

Graph 14 shows the percent of alcohol in the blood of 454 felonious homicide victims. An examination of this figure reveals that 36.6 percent of the victims were in the second, third, and fourth stages of intoxication, and were, therefore, definitely under the influence of alcohol. The stages of alcoholic intoxication are explained in Table 30. An additional 12.8 percent of the victims had, as revealed by blood tests, been drinking, but were within the first stage, or "safe" zone, of intoxication, and cannot be labeled as definitely under the influence of alcohol. There were also 31 cases (6.8 percent) in which the victims lived too long after the assault for a blood alcohol test to be made. Normal dissipation rate of alcohol in blood requires tests to be made within 24 hours after the assault. There was evidence in these 31 cases that the victims had been drinking, but the extent of their drinking is not known.

On the other side, the blood alcohol tests of 148 victims, or 32.6 percent, were negative. And in 11.2 percent of the cases, while again the victims lived too long for tests to be made, there was no evidence that they had been drinking.

Blood tests are not made in the cases of persons accused of committing felonious homicides. The only evidence is that obtained by the police in the questioning of the accused and whatever witnesses there may have been. This evidence indicated that in approximately 40 percent of the cases the accused slayers had been drinking.

Since, however, the questions principally were of the type: "Was the accused intoxicated?" or, "Had the accused been drinking?" the answers rarely gave a reasonably accurate indication of the extent of the presence of alcohol. As a result, this evidence is of questionable value.

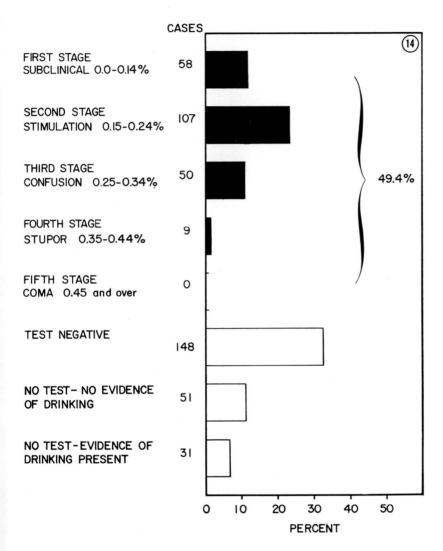

Graph 14. Stages of Intoxication—Victims of Felonious Homicide.

A word of caution is, perhaps, proper. It is not the extent of the *presence* of alcohol that is important. It is the extent to which alcohol is a *contributing factor*. Unfortunately, the latter cannot be measured clinically. One cannot read the cases, however, without concluding that, in a majority of felonious homicides, the pres-

94 *HOMICIDE IN AN URBAN COMMUNITY*

ence of alcohol in substantial quantities made the discords more acute than they otherwise would have been. Alcohol set the stage for the tragedy which followed!

TABLE 30

STAGES OF ALCOHOL INTOXICATION

(Under Influence of Alcohol)

Stage	Blood	Urine	Clinical Symptoms
Subclinical (Note over-lapping)	0.01%-0.12%	0.01%-0.16%	2 oz. whiskey or 2 bottles of beer by AVERAGE person. No apparent intoxication. Feeling good, increased self-confidence; NORMAL by ordinary observation, slight changes by special tests. (30% of people will be "intoxicated.")
Stimulation (Note over-lapping)	0.09%-0.21%	0.13%-0.29%	6 to 7 oz. of whiskey or 6 to 7 bottles of beer by AVERAGE person. Impaired memory, comprehension and lack of critical judgment; decreased inhibition, slight incoordination. Slowing of stimuli response.
Confusion (Note over-lapping)	0.18%-0.30%	0.26%-0.42%	Acute intoxication, advanced symptoms of drunkenness; muscular incoordination, staggering gait, dizziness, slurred speech and sensory disturbances.
Stupor (Note over-lapping)	0.27%-0.39%	0.38%-0.54%	Apathy, general inertia and approaching paralysis, marked stimuli decrease and impaired consciousness.
Coma (Note over-lapping)	0.36%-0.48%	0.51%-0.67%	Complete unconsciousness, subnormal temperature, depressed and abolished reflexes, anaesthesia, impaired circulation, weak pulse, stertorous breathing. Possible death.

These correlations prepared for and accepted by the National Safety Council Committee on Tests for Intoxication.

The term "under the influence of alcohol" should be used instead of "intoxication." *Every* person is influenced by 0.15% alcohol in the blood.

"Average" person is a normal individual weighing about 150 pounds. Reaction is colored by individual's personality.

Photograph 9. A true symbol of homicide. The victim with 0.31% blood alcohol grasps the bar stool. Over one-half the victims had alcohol present in their body.

B. JUSTIFIABLE HOMICIDES

As shown by Graph 15, 40.8 percent of the 157 decedents justifiably slain were in the second, third, and fourth stages of intoxication, and were, therefore, definitely under the influence of alcohol at the times of their decease. An additional 15.9 percent, blood tests indicated, had been drinking, but were within the so-called "safe" zone, and cannot be labeled as definitely under the influence of alcohol. Evidence also indicated that 6 decedents (3.8 percent) had been drinking, but these persons lived too long after the assaults for blood tests to be made, and the extent of their drinking is not known. Upon adding these percentages, it is found that there was some evidence of drinking in 60.5 percent of the cases.

Photograph 10. Alcohol can also be an important element in homicides at home. This living room scene indicated a friendly family group.

Photograph 11. The family group of photograph 10 in bed. Mother and daughter are homicide victims with no alcohol present in either. The father-slayer, a suicide, with blood alcohol 0.07% and urine alcohol 0.14%.

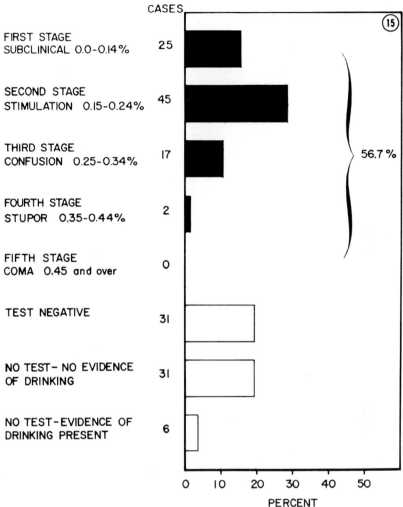

Graph 15. Stages of Intoxication—Justifiable Homicide Victims.

The blood alcohol tests of 31 persons, or 19.7 percent, showed no alcohol. In another 31 cases, although no tests were made because the persons lived too long, there was no evidence that the decedents had been drinking.

With the exception of the cases in which the slayers were police officers, one might well assume that some of the slayers were intoxicated. Unfortunately, the available records did not contain this information.

Chapter XI

SUMMARY

1. A total of 662 homicides occurred in Cuyahoga County, Ohio, between January 1, 1947 and December 31, 1953.

(a) One hundred fifty-seven deaths were ruled justifiable homicides.

(b) The alleged slayers of 454 persons were charged with felonious homicides: *i.e.,* murder in the first or second degree, or manslaughter in the first degree.

(c) Fifty-one homicides are listed as unclassified homicides. (This category consists chiefly of unsolved cases and cases in which the slayers committed suicide before charges could be brought against them.)

2. There appeared to be no relationship between homicide and the months or seasons of the year.

3. Homicide varied with the days of the week. Fridays, Saturdays, and Sundays accounted for 62.3 percent of the homicides during the seven years surveyed.

4. Over 60 percent of all homicidal assaults took place between 6:01 P.M. and 3:00 A.M.

5. The police of Cuyahoga County, Ohio apprehended the alleged assailants in 95.5 percent of the cases.

6. Of all defendants who were either found not guilty without qualification, or who were convicted of some criminal offense: 26.3 percent were convicted as originally charged by indictment; 45.5 percent were convicted of lesser offenses; and 28.2 percent were found not guilty without qualification and released.

7. Of all defendants convicted as originally charged by indictment, 24.2 percent pleaded guilty. Of those convicted of lesser offenses, 50.9 percent pleaded guilty. Thus, of all defendants convicted of some type criminal offense, 41.1 percent pleaded guilty.

8. Thirty-eight percent of all persons standing trial waived

HOMICIDE IN AN URBAN COMMUNITY

trial by jury and elected to be tried by court. Forty-three percent of these defendants were found not guilty; 38.6 percent of those tried by a jury were found not guilty and released.

9. Mercy was recommended in 72.7 percent of the cases in which the defendants were convicted of murder in the first degree.

10. Approximately 17 percent of all persons convicted of offenses other than murder, and who, therefore, were eligible, received suspended sentences and were placed upon probation.

11. Approximately 76 percent of all persons accused of committing felonious homicides were members of the Negro race. In 1950, members of the Negro race made up 16.2 percent of the population of the City of Cleveland, and 10.7 percent of the population of Cuyahoga County, Ohio.

12. On the whole, there were no significant differences with respect to the disposition of the cases of white and Negro persons accused of felonious homicides.

13. Women accounted for only 13.9 percent of all persons accused of felonious homicides.

14. The over-all conviction rate for men was approximately 10 percent higher than the rate for women. However, 40 percent of all eligible women convicts were placed upon probation; as compared to 13 percent of the eligible male convicts.

15. Approximately 25 percent of all males accused of felonious homicides were charged with slaying females.

16. Approximately 81 percent of all females accused of felonious homicides were charged with slaying males.

17. Persons accused of felonious homicides were relatively young. Seventy-two percent were within the ages of 21 through 45.

18. One hundred twenty-two persons were justifiably slain by private citizens. Approximately 79 percent of the decedents were Negroes.

19. Thirty-five persons were justifiably slain by police officers. Approximately 74 percent of the decedents were Negroes.

20. The decedents in the cases of justifiable homicide were also relatively young; 80.6 percent were within the ages of 16 through 45.

21. Firearms were used in over 55 percent of all homicides

involving private citizens. Cutting and piercing instruments were employed in nearly 25 percent of the cases.

22. Thirty-six percent of the felonious homicide victims were under the influence of alcohol at the time they were assaulted. It is estimated that at least the same percentage of persons accused of committing felonious homicides were under the influence of alcohol.

23. Forty percent of the decedents who were justifiably slain were under the influence of alcohol.

24. With the exception of justifiable homicides committed by police officers, for the most part, all type homicides involved members of the same race. That is, Negroes killed Negroes and whites killed whites.

25. The situations out of which homicides most frequently arose were: (1) quarrels of a mostly petty nature; (2) marital discords in which one spouse killed the other; and (3) love or sex disputes in which the deceased was slain by one other than his spouse or "common law" mate.

SOCIAL ASPECTS OF URBAN HOMICIDE

INTRODUCTION

The social and economic data on which the following tables and graphs are based were derived—unless otherwise indicated—from the *United States 1950 Census of Population,* Bulletin P-012, a U. S. Department of Commerce publication, or from *Measuring Leisure Time Needs* by Virginia K. White, a 1954 publication of the Group Work Council, Welfare Federation of Cleveland. The latter, in turn, derived most of its data from the U. S. Census. Other sources are noted therein.

Fortunate for the relevance (and, therefore, accuracy) of the data, the United States Census of 1950 took place at the mid-point of the seven-year period covered by this study. It is reasonably safe to assume that the various social indices changed at a continuous rate during the seven years, and that the 1950 figures reflect the average for the seven years. In some cases, the dates are for 1953. The reader should take this into account in studying them.

The graphs, tables and maps tell more than is brought out in the comments which precede and follow them. These comments represent an attempt to draw the reader's attention to the salient features of the particular set of data. The interested reader is urged to study the graphic and tabular data with care and to note the various deviations from the general pattern. They may be of considerable significance.

In the seven-year period 1947-1953 there occurred in Cuyahoga County 662 homicides. Where in the county did these homicides occur? Were they concentrated in a few areas, or evenly distributed throughout the county? Where did the assailants live? Where did their victims live? To answer these questions—will reveal the incidence and distribution of homicide in terms of the *kinds of neighborhoods* in which it tends to occur. Do neighborhoods produce murderers? Or do other factors incite homicide?

Certain generalizations underlie the study: first, that homicide is a social phenomenon and that a high or low incidence of homicide is one index among others of the social health of the area;

second, that poorer neighborhoods, run-down, slum-type areas, would show a higher incidence of homicide than richer, newer areas; third, that the incidence of homicide would correlate rather highly with the other social indices.

Since these generalizations existed before the study was commenced, every effort was made not to let them exert an undue influence on the selection of data and on their presentation. The generalizations served as working hypotheses. They have been examined in the cold light of statistical fact.

It must be constantly borne in mind, in studying the data which follow, that social phenomena are complex. If it be shown, for example, that a high incidence of homicide exists where housing is substandard and over-crowded—this association of the two factors—homicide and poor housing do not necessarily establish a cause and effect relationship. If the presence of fact A is associated with the presence of fact B, various inferences suggest themselves. They may be causally related. They may both be the effect of some other factor which is the cause. Or their association may be the result of chance or coincidence.

Even if there *is* a causal relationship, it may not be direct or immediate. Factor A may interact with numerous other factors in producing some new factor which in turn interacts with still other factors to produce factor B. Obviously, the mere presence of A does not permit us to predict that B will be present as well.

Statistics is merely a method of presenting the facts. It is not a formula for ultimate truth. With these precautions suggested, a description of method is in order.

To locate homicides it is necessary to divide the county into areas. Fortunately a convenient division has been made by The Group Work Council of the Welfare Federation of Cleveland. The county has been divided into 42 Social Planning Areas, each constituting as much as possible a homogeneous area with a homogeneous population. Twenty-eight of the Areas are in the City of Cleveland and 14 in the suburbs. Appendix A indicates the census tracts included in each Social Planning Area.

Chapter I

THE DISTRIBUTION OF HOMICIDE—MURDER IS CONCENTRATED

The most conspicuous fact about the geographical distribution of homicide is its extraordinarily high concentration in a few areas. Sixty-two percent of the 655 homicides for which the scene was ascertained occurred in three contiguous areas: Central-West, Central and Central-East.

Why do almost two-thirds of all homicides occur in only 0.6% of the county's population (12% of the City of Cleveland)?

Homicides did occur in 35 of the 42 Social Planning Areas. But only ten areas had 10 or more homicides. These ten areas accounted for 571 of the 655 homicides whose scenes were known. And even among these top 10 areas the range was immense, from

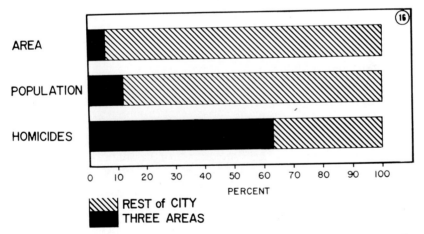

Graph 16. Percentage of Homicides in the City of Cleveland Occurring in the Three Social Planning Areas with the Highest Rate of Homicide (Central-West, Central, and Central-East Areas). Percentage of the City's Area Which These Three Areas Constitute. Percentage of the City's Population Living in These Three Areas.

105

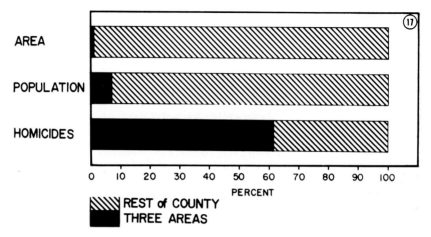

Graph 17. Percentage of County's Homicides Occurring in the Three Social Planning Areas (Central-West, Central, and Central-East) with the Highest Rate of Homicide. Portion of the County's Area Which These Three Areas Constitute. Portion of the County's Population Living in These Three Areas.

235 (Central-West) to 13 (North Broadway). Seven areas had between 5 and 10 homicides, and eighteen areas had between 1 and 5. It will be noted that the number of homicides which occur in a given area coincides fairly closely with the number of assailants and victims. If the addresses of all assailants and victims were known, the coincidence might be still greater. This does not conclusively establish that most assailants kill people in their own neighborhoods, but it certainly points to the probability of that being the case.

When it is noted that most homicides are manslaughter, (crimes of outburst) rather than murders (premeditated malice or killings while committing robbery), the fact that they are, for the most part, committed in the assailant's own area is not surprising.

The most irregular distribution of homicide makes it difficult either to apply any of the common statistical devices or to present the entire body of data in a valid and graphic fashion. For example, Central-West and Downtown are both in the highest quintile as to number of homicides;[1] yet the former area has more than ten

---
[1] See Map 3.

HOMICIDE IN AN URBAN COMMUNITY

TABLE 31

TABULAR SUMMARY OF GRAPH 16

Social Planning Area	Area (net acres)	% of the City's Area	Popula- tion	% of the City's Popula- tion	Number of Homi- cides	% of the City's Homi- cides
Central—West	759	2.5	49,534	5.4	235	36.8
Central	408	1.3	25,722	2.8	113	17.7
Central—East	644	2.1	37,696	4.1	60	9.4
- - - - - - - -	- - - - -	- - - - -	- - - - -	- - - - -	- - - - -	- - - - -
Total of the 3 Areas	1811	5.9	112,952	12.3	408	63.9
The entire city	30,740	100.0	914,808	100.0	639	100.0
The city ex- cluding the 3 areas	28,929	94.1	801,856	87.7	231	36.1

TABLE 32

TABULAR SUMMARY OF GRAPH 17

Social Planning Area	Area in Net Acres	% of the County's Area	Popula- tion	% of the County's Popula- tion	No. of Homi- cides	% of the County's Homi- cides
Central—West	759	0.3	49,534	3.6	235	35.5
Central	408	0.1	25,722	1.8	113	17.1
Central—East	644	0.2	37,696	2.7	60	9.1
Totals of the three areas	1811	0.6	112,952	8.1	408	61.7
The Entire County	278,952	100.0	1,389,532	100.0	662	100.0
The County excluding the three social planning areas	277,141	99.4	1,276,580	91.9	254	38.3

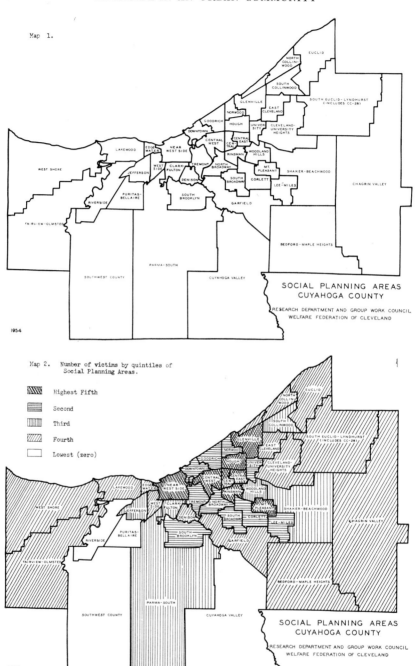

Map 1.

Map 2. Number of victims by quintiles of Social Planning Areas.

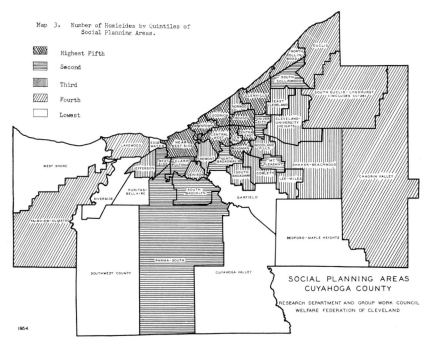

Map 3. Number of Homicides by Quintiles of Social Planning Areas.

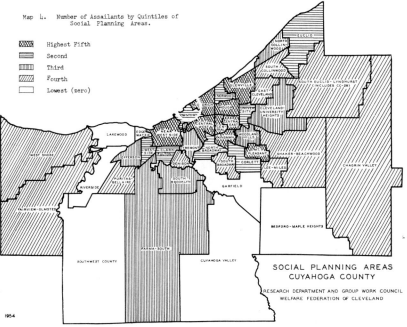

Map 4. Number of Assailants by Quintiles of Social Planning Areas.

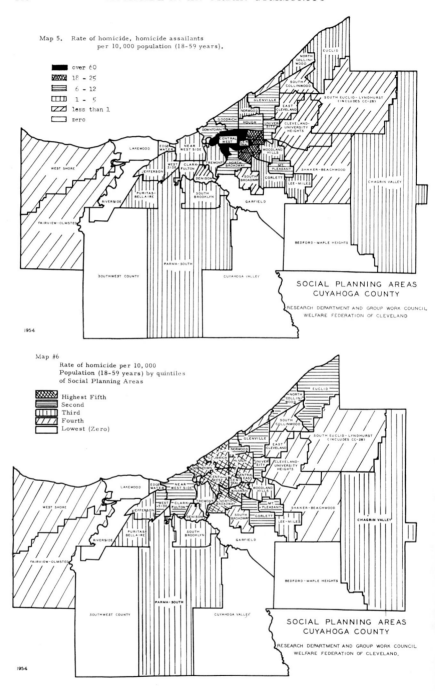

Map 5. Rate of homicide, homicide assailants per 10,000 population (18-59 years).

Map #6 Rate of homicide per 10,000 Population (18-59 years) by quintiles of Social Planning Areas

TABLE 33

NUMBER OF HOMICIDES, NUMBER OF ASSAILANTS AND NUMBER OF VICTIMS, THE SCENES OR ADDRESSES OF WHICH ARE KNOWN

Area	Scenes	Assailants	Victims
1. Central	113	104	123
2. Central—East	60	63	74
3. Central—West	235	204	193
4. Clark-Fulton	6	7	4
5. Corlett	4	10	8
6. Denison	1	1	1
7. Downtown	21	6	14
8. Edgewater	0	0	3
9. Glenville	31	33	34
10. Goodrich	19	12	11
11. Hough	27	31	29
12. Jefferson	4	3	5
13. Kinsman	35	24	27
14. Lee-Miles	0	0	1
15. Mount Pleasant	7	15	15
16. Near West Side	17	14	20
17. North Broadway	13	9	12
18. North Collinwood	1	4	2
19. Norwood	4	8	6
20. Puritas-Bellaire	0	1	0
21. Riverside	0	0	0
22. South Broadway	3	2	6
23. South Brooklyn	5	4	6
24. South Collinwood	5	1	5
25. Tremont	4	3	6
26. University	9	7	7
27. West Side	5	7	3
28. Woodland Hills	3	3	4
City Total	632	576	619
29. Bedford-Maple Heights	0	0	1
30. Chagrin Valley	1	1	1
31. Cleveland-University Heights	3	3	3
32. Cuyahoga Valley	0	0	0
33. East Cleveland	3	1	3
34. Euclid	2	6	2
35. Fairview-Olmsted	2	1	1
36. Garfield	1	0	1
37. Lakewood	2	0	2
38. Parma-South	5	4	4
39. Shaker-Beechwood	3	1	4
40. South Euclid-Lyndhurst	1	1	1
41. Southwest City	0	0	0
42. West Shore	0	1	2
Suburban Total	23	19	25
County Total	655	595	644

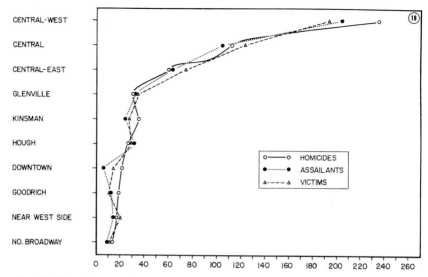

Graph 18. The Ten Social Planning Areas with the Greatest Number of Homicides. Comparison of the Number of Homicides Which Occurred in Each Area with the Number of Assailants and Victims Who Lived There. (Some assailants' and victims' addresses were not available.)

times as many as the latter. Moreover, the numerical gap among the ten high areas is far greater than that between the lowest of them and the areas with the least incidence of homicide.[2]

The most valuable analysis can be made only if the areas with the highest number of homicides are considered and their "social statistics" compared, among themselves and as a group, with the areas which had few homicides or none. Because of the extreme skewness of the distribution, only by comparing the extremes can any worthwhile conclusion be drawn.

HOMICIDE RATE

The finding that homicides are concentrated in a few areas remains unchanged if the crude geographic incidence is compared to population density incidence. For purposes other than comparison there is, of course, value in noting where the largest number

---

[2]See Table 33 and Map 3.

HOMICIDE IN AN URBAN COMMUNITY

of homicides occurred and where most assailants and victims originated. But for valid comparison one must utilize some index which takes population differences into account. The "homicide rate" is such an index. It measures the number of assailants per 10,000 population over the seven year period of study in proportion to the population living in the area at the midpoint in time of the period of study, the 1950 census. Since the vast majority of homicides were committed by persons over 18 and under 60, it was thought wise to exclude from the population persons below 18 and 60 or over in computing the homicide rate. Whatever shortcomings it may have from the viewpoint of scientific precision, the index does seem to provide a fair basis for rough comparison.[3]

The same problem of skewness presents itself when using rates as in the case of comparing the absolute number of homicides, though less acutely. There are still several areas with a rate of zero. The ten most "homicidal" areas demonstrate the problem. Their homicide rates are as follows:

72.2	9.6
62.1	7.6
24.1	7.3
18.1	6.3
11.9	6.2

The highest rate, it will be noted, is thirteen times as great as that of the tenth ranking area, while the tenth is only some five times as high as the twenty-fifth (which has a rate of 1.1). The gaps are large at the top and small at the bottom. This makes the quintile maps somewhat deceptive to the unwary, for they fail to disclose that the range within the highest quintile is much greater than in the others.

ETHNIC AND RACIAL DISTRIBUTION

Homicides were most prevalent in areas populated by Negroes and least prevalent in areas predominantly native-born white.

---

[3]If R = homicide rate; P = population 18-59 years of age; and N = number of assailants who lived in the area, the formula for computing the homicide rate is:

$$R = \frac{10,000\,N}{P}$$

TABLE 34

HOMICIDE RATE OF THE 42 SOCIAL PLANNING AREAS
(Listed alphabetically)

Area	Population 18 - 59	Number of Assailants	Rate per 10,000
1. Central	16,751	104	62.1
2. Central—East	26,111	63	24.1
3. Central—West	28,235	204	72.2
4. Clark-Fulton	15,295	7	4.6
5. Corlett	25,617	10	3.9
6. Denison	13,716	1	0.7
7. Downtown	6,231	6	9.6
8. Edgewater	7,049	0	0
9. Glenville	52,246	33	6.3
10. Goodrich	10,113	12	11.9
11. Hough	42,555	31	7.3
12. Jefferson	19,192	3	1.6
13. Kinsman	12,181	22	18.1
14. Lee-Miles	10,926	2	1.9
15. Mount Pleasant	24,090	15	6.2
16. Near West Side	38,480	14	3.6
17. North Broadway	11,870	9	7.6
18. North Collinwood	16,894	4	2.4
19. Norwood	17,427	8	4.6
20. Puritas-Bellaire	10,189	1	1.0
21. Riverside	15,212	0	0
22. South Broadway	25,133	2	0.8
23. South Brooklyn	24,520	4	1.6
24. South Collinwood	20,353	1	0.5
25. Tremont	17,577	3	1.7
26. University	12,081	7	5.8
27. West Side	16,741	7	4.2
28. Woodland Hills	27,110	3	1.1
City Total	*565,895*	*576*	*10.2*
29. Bedford-Maple Heights	18,157	0	0
30. Chagrin Valley	6,091	1	1.6
31. Cleveland-University Heights	42,120	3	0.7
32. Cuyahoga Valley	5,262	0	0
33. East Cleveland	24,986	1	0.4
34. Euclid	24,563	6	2.4
35. Fairview-Olmsted	12,062	1	0.8
36. Garfield	16,100	0	0
37. Lakewood	40,959	0	0
38. Parma-South	27,273	4	1.5
39. Shaker-Beechwood	21,628	1	0.5
40. South Euclid-Lyndhurst	19,354	1	0.5
41. Southwest City	11,945	0	0
42. West Shore	13,581	1	0.7
Suburban Total	*284,081*	*19*	*0.7*
Cuyahoga County	849,976	595	7.0

HOMICIDE IN AN URBAN COMMUNITY

TABLE 35

HOMICIDE RATE OF THE SOCIAL PLANNING AREAS—ARRANGED BY QUINTILES

(APPROXIMATE)

	Area	Homicide Rate
First Quintile	Central-West	72.2
	Central	62.1
	Central-East	24.1
	Kinsman	18.1
	Goodrich	11.9
	Downtown	9.6
	North Broadway	7.6
	Hough	7.3
Second Quintile	Glenville	6.3
	Mount Pleasant	6.2
	University	5.8
	Norwood	4.6
	Clark-Fulton	4.6
	West Side	4.2
	Corlett	3.9
	Near West Side	3.6
	Euclid	2.4
	North Collinwood	2.4
Third Quintile	Lee-Miles	1.9
	Tremont	1.7
	Chagrin Valley	1.6
	South Brooklyn	1.6
	Jefferson	1.6
	Parma-South	1.5
	Woodland Hills	1.1
	Puritas-Bellaire	1.0
Fourth Quintile	Fairview-Olmsted	0.8
	South Broadway	0.8
	West Shore	0.7
	Cleveland-University Heights	0.7
	Denison	0.7
	South Euclid-Lyndhurst	0.5
	Shaker-Beechwood	0.5
	South Collinwood	0.5
	East Cleveland	0.4
Fifth Quintile	Southwest County	0
	Lakewood	0
	Garfield	0
	Cuyahoga Valley	0
	Bedford-Maple Heights	0
	Riverside	0
	Edgewater	0

116   HOMICIDE IN AN URBAN COMMUNITY

Seventy-six percent of the population of Cuyahoga County was native white on April 1, 1950; 13% was foreign-born white; 11% was non-white (primarily Negroes, a few Orientals).

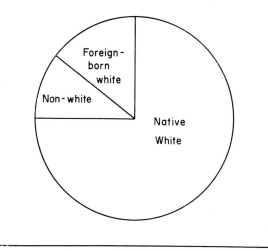

1950 - Population of Cuyahoga County

The percentages are somewhat different if only the adult population (21 years old and over) be considered.

But in only eight social planning areas did non-white persons constitute 10% or more of the population.

All of these areas were in the upper half of the areas ranked according to homicide rate. Four were in the first quintile; the other four areas in the first quintile have smaller percentages of non-white population than does the city as a whole. The fact

TABLE 36

PERCENTAGES OF ADULT POPULATION (21 YEARS AND OLDER)

	Native White	Foreign-Born White	Non-White
Cuyahoga County	70.7	18.8	10.5
City of Cleveland	64.1	20.4	15.5

TABLE 37

Area	Per Cent of Population Non-White
Central	95.3
Central-East	81.7
Central-West	77.2
Kinsman	52.0
Glenville	25.1
Mt. Pleasant	22.2
Lee-Miles	18.8
University	10.8

remains that the three areas which account for over 60% of the homicides, which were also the three areas with the highest *rate* of homicide, were the three areas with the highest concentration of non-white population.

This is not to suggest that the Negroes as a race possess some super-homicidal tendency. It *is* to suggest, however, that the Negroes live, for the most part, in those areas of greatest social

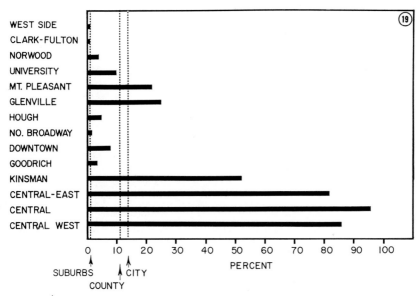

Graph 19. Percentage of Population Which Is Non-white in the 14 Areas with the Highest Rate of Homicide.

TABLE 38

TABULAR SUMMARY OF GRAPH 19. PERCENTAGE OF POPULATION WHICH IS NON-WHITE IN 14 SOCIAL PLANNING AREAS

Area	Percentage of Population Non-White
West Side	0.1
Clark-Fulton	0.1
Norwood	4.2
University	10.4
Mount Pleasant	22.2
Glenville	25.1
Hough	4.9
North Broadway	1.1
Downtown	8.0
Goodrich	3.1
Kinsman	52.0
Central-East	81.7
Central	95.3
Central-West	87.2

need, poorest health, and most sub-standard housing, which characteristics (as will be seen) correlate so highly with the homicide rate. It is also to suggest that they, on the whole, acquire less formal education and earn less money than the general population, factors which may also play a role in producing those tensions and needs which tend to explode into homicides.

Chapter II

SOCIO-ECONOMIC CONDITIONS IN HOMICIDE AREAS

MEDIAN FAMILY INCOME

The lower the income, the greater the homicide rate! Graph 20 represents the median family income in 21 of the 42 areas, namely the seven with the highest rate of homicide, the seven with the next highest rate, and the seven with a rate of zero—no homicide assailants.

The median family income for the city, the suburbs, and the county as a whole are shown as an additional standard of comparison.

A cursory glance at the graph will disclose that these three groups of social planning areas rank as groups in the same order in income as they do in homicide rates. There are individual differences, but the group picture is definite and vivid. The areas in the first two groups are arranged in descending order of homicide rate. A perfect correlation with income (i.e., low income yielding high homicide rate) would show an ascending order of income. And this is the case, with the exception of two areas: Downtown and University. The former has too low an income for its homicide rate (or too high a homicide rate for its income); the latter is in the opposite situation. These "imperfections" in the correlation are somewhat reconciled, however, for these two areas are quite generally considered atypical. By their very nature as Downtown (largely hotel and commercial) and University areas respectively, and the abnormal heterogeneity of their populations, they are set apart as unique.[4]

With these two areas omitted, the progression from high

---

[4]In calculating the various indices of social need in "Measuring Leisure Time Needs" the Downtown area was excluded from consideration. The University area should probably have been excluded too.

HOMICIDE IN AN URBAN COMMUNITY

TABLE 39

TABULAR SUMMARY OF GRAPH 20: MEDIAN FAMILY INCOME (1949)

Area		
Central-West	$2051.50	
Central	2369.50	
Central-East	2703.00	
Kinsman	2941.00	
Goodrich	3250.00	
Downtown	2691.00	
North Broadway	3407.00	
Hough	3332.50	City of Cleveland—$3539.00
Glenville	3560.00	
Mt. Pleasant	3506.00	Suburbs—$4772.00
University	4175.00	
Norwood	3716.00	Cuyahoga County—$3971.00
Clark-Fulton	3857.00	
West Side	3929.00	
Edgewater	4311.50	
Riverside	4605.00	
Bedford-Maple Hts.	4095.00	
Cuyahoga Valley	4451.00	
Garfield	4269.50	
Lakewood	4730.00	
Southwest County	4118.00	

homicide areas to low is a steady progression from low income to high. Thus, one of the original generalizations seems to be borne out.

The fluctuation among the seven areas in the last group is not significant. All of these areas had a homicide rate of zero; they could have been arranged in any order. What *is* significant is the fact that all of these areas are—in their median income—above the city and county medians.

One might experience some surprise upon noting that the four areas which exceed the suburban median were not among

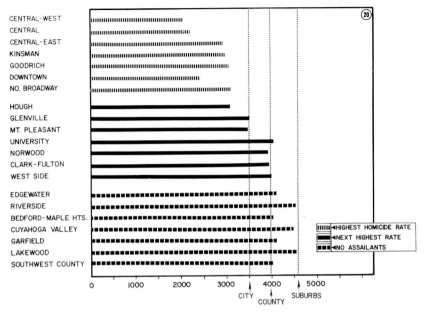

Graph 20. Median Family Income (in dollars per year) (1949).

those with a homicide rate of zero. These areas and their median incomes are set forth below:

TABLE 40

Area	Median Family Income
Shaker-Beechwood	$7423.00
Cleveland-University Hts.	5958.00
West Shore	5540.00
South Euclid-Lyndhurst	4938.50

These rates are so close to zero that there is no significant difference between the homicidality of these areas and of the seven in group three of Graph 20.

With the exception of the abnormal University area, all of the areas in group two are below the county median, but nearly all are well above the city median.

HOMICIDE IN AN URBAN COMMUNITY

They were the four areas with the highest median family incomes. Their homicide rates were as follows:

TABLE 41

Area	Homicide Rate
Shaker-Beechwood	0.5
Cleveland-University Hts.	0.7
West Shore	0.7
South Euclid-Lyndhurst	0.5

None of the most homicidal areas is above the city median in income.

One additional point ought to be made. The absolute differences in income seem to be relatively small when compared with the differences in homicide rate. For example, the homicide rate of Central—West is 10 times that of Hough, while the rate of their median family incomes is only 1 to 1.6. The range in income distribution is relatively small. To draw from this the conclusion, that the real difference in income between areas with extreme differences in homicide rate is quite insignificant, is to make a serious error, for the difference between an income of $2051 (Central—West) and an income of $3332 (Hough) is greater than the mere arithmetical difference. Without considering the cost of living, it may be pointed out that the lower of these incomes may not be sufficient to pay for the bare necessities of family life, while the greater of them may adequately cover necessities and leave enough for those luxuries and amenities which make for some degree of comfort in the home. The difference between these two statuses or abilities is the real index of social significance, rather than the mere ratio of incomes. Moreover, family income is being studied and the size of the family which the income must support has not been taken into account. It is generally known that families in the lower income brackets (and lower education levels) tend to be larger. When this fact is thrown into the balance, it increases the true gap in income between the "homicide prone" areas and the areas with the lowest rate.

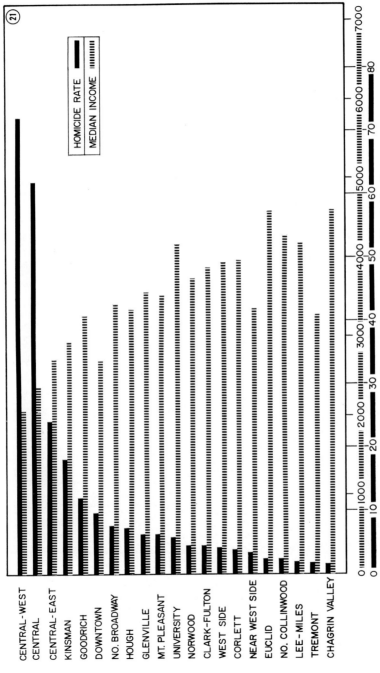

Graph 21. Median Family Income in Dollars per Year as Compared with Homicide Rate.

(21) cont'd.

SO. BROOKLYN
JEFFERSON
PARMA-SOUTH
WOODLAND HILLS
PURITAS-BELL
FAIRVIEW-OLMSTED
SO. BROADWAY
WEST SHORE
CLEVE.-UNIV. HTS.
DENISON
SO. EUCLID-LYNDHURST
SHAKER-BEACHWOOD
SO. COLLINWOOD
EAST CLEVELAND
SOUTHWEST CITY
LAKEWOOD
GARFIELD HTS.
CUYAHOGA VALLEY
BEDFORD-MAPLE HTS.
RIVERSIDE
EDGEWATER

7423.

0   1000   2000   3000   4000   5000   6000   7000
0   10   20   30   40   50   60   70   80

EDUCATION: MORE EDUCATION—LESS HOMICIDE!

Two indices to portray the educational level of the various areas: median years of schooling completed and percentage of the population which has had no high school. In both cases, only the population 25 years of age and older was considered, on the assumption that formal schooling has, by that age, been completed.

The graphs have been set up in the same manner as that of the median family income—the 14 areas with the highest homicide rate have been ranked in a descending order by homicide rate and divided into two groups of seven. These groups have been compared with the seven areas whose homicide rate was zero. All have been compared with the city, the suburbs, and the county as a whole.

The picture presented by the first graph is quite similar to that given by the income graph. This is not surprising because of the long-recognized fact that income correlates highly with education.

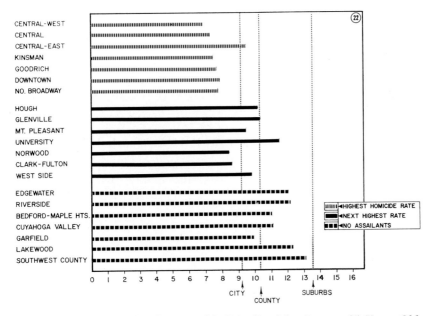

Graph 22. Median Schooling (Grade) Completed by Persons 25 Years Old and Over (1950).

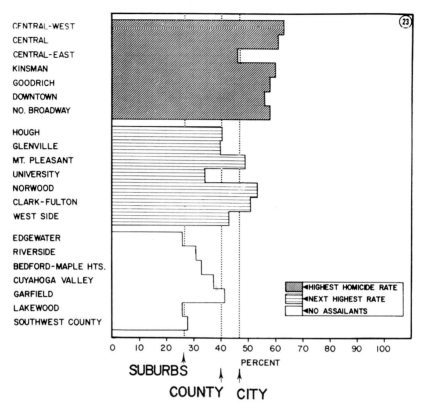

Graph 23. Percentage of Population 25 Years Old and Over Which Has Had No High School (1950).

The first group of seven areas lies consistently below the city median and except for Central–East, *well* below it. The second group, except for the atypical University area, is distributed around the city median, ranging from a year below it, to a year above it. The third group lies, for the most part, well above the county median.

Again, the very highest-ranking areas have a positive homicide rate but, except for Chagrin Valley, less than 1. They belong, to all practical intents, in the group of zero-rate areas.

The second graph, representing the percentage of the population which has not had any high school education, presents, as expected, an inverted picture. The areas with the highest homicide

TABLE 42

EDUCATION OF POPULATION 25 YEARS OLD AND OVER:
TABULAR SUMMARY OF GRAPHS 22 AND 23

Area	Per Cent with No High School	Median Grade Completed
Central—West	63.5	6.99
Central	61.6	7.30
Central—East	46.9	9.39
Kinsman	60.6	7.43
Goodrich	58.7	7.66
Downtown	56.7	7.94
North Broadway	58.3	7.73
Hough	40.7	10.29
Glenville	40.6	10.36
Mt. Pleasant	49.1	9.13
University	34.1	11.69
Norwood	53.5	8.41
Clark-Fulton	51.8	8.68
West Side	43.9	9.84
Edgewater	27.7	12.07
Riverside	30.1	12.05
Bedford-Maple Heights	33.8	10.98
Cuyahoga Valley	37.4	11.15
Garfield	42.9	9.92
Lakewood	26.4	12.25
Southwest County	28.4	13.10
City of Cleveland	47.2	9.39
Suburbs	27.3	13.7
County	40.3	10.40

rate have the largest proportion of persons who did not reach high school. It is somewhat surprising to see how large a percentage of the population fits into the no-high school category in such areas as Garfield and Cuyahoga Valley. Obviously that factor alone does not induce homicide.

The same precaution should be taken in interpreting these graphs as in the case of income. The difference between a median 6.99 (Central—West) years of schooling and a median 12.25 (Lake-

128 *HOMICIDE IN AN URBAN COMMUNITY*

TABLE 43

AREAS WITH MOST EDUCATION

Area	Median Years of Education	Homicide Rate
Shaker-Beechwood	12.72	0.5
Cleveland-University Heights	12.53	0.7
West Shore	12.51	0.7
Chagrin Valley	12.38	1.6
South Euclid-Lyndhurst	12.25	0.5

wood) seems small; one is less than twice the other. But a little reflection will show that the real difference is tremendous. Medians are only indices of the point which divides the top half from the bottom half. They are not an indication (except in a perfect, bell-shaped distribution curve) of the extent to which the cases cluster around the mid-point. For example, the median grade completed in Central—West was 6.99. This means that half the adult population completed more than that and half less. It does not tell us how many of those who completed less had only two or three years, and how many had six years of school. Similarly, Lakewood's median is 12.25. But how many completed college? In fact 26.2% of Lakewood's adults (25 years or over) had some college, and 14.6% completed college. In Central—West 5.5% had some college education and 2.3% had completed college. The difference, then, between a median of 6.99 and one of 12.25 becomes more significant. And when one realizes that education is a key to job and income, to further informal education through reading, attendance at cultural events, and to participation in communal activities, the difference takes on true importance.

OCCUPATIONAL DISTRIBUTION: THE LOWER THE OCCUPATIONAL STATUS, THE HIGHER THE HOMICIDE RATE!

Closely connected with both income and education is the occupational distribution of the employed persons in an area. The

United States Census utilizes nine occupation groups:
- A. Professional, technical and kindred workers.
    Managers, officials, and proprietors (including farm).
- B. Clerical and kindred workers.
    Sales workers.
    Craftsmen, foremen, and kindred workers.
- C. Private household workers.
    Service workers, except private household
    Laborers.

This study has arranged them in three groups of descending "status." Graphs 24 and 25 portray the percentage of the labor force in each of the top-most homicidal areas in the A and C categories respectively.

The deviations from generalization should be noted and studied. It can be seen that, generally speaking, as the proportion of workers in the occupations of least status (Class C) increases, the homicide rate increases also. In the second graph it can be seen that the converse is true in the case of the highest class occupations. That is, the most homicidal areas have, with some deviations, a

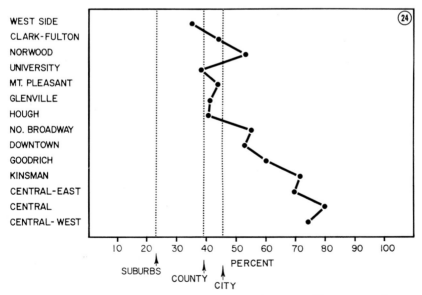

Graph 24. Percentage of Employed Persons in Non-skilled Occupations.

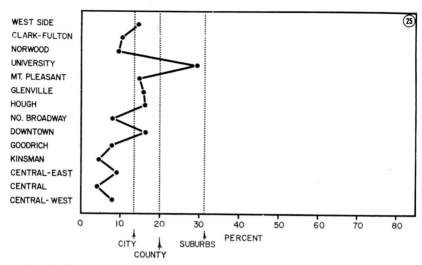

Graph 25. Percentage of Employed Persons Employed in Managerial or Professional Work.

TABLE 44

Tabular Summary of Graphs 24 and 25: Occupational Distribution

Area	A Per Cent Managerial and Professional	B Per Cent Clerical Sales and Crafts	Total A and B	Per Cent Others
West Side	14.2	50.4	64.6	35.4
Clark-Fulton	10.4	45.4	55.8	44.2
Norwood	9.4	38.6	48.0	52.0
University	29.5	33.8	63.3	36.7
Mt. Pleasant	14.3	40.9	55.2	44.8
Glenville	15.4	41.2	56.6	43.4
Hough	16.1	42.2	58.3	41.7
North Broadway	7.9	37.6	45.5	54.5
Downtown	16.3	30.8	47.1	52.9
Goodrich	7.8	31.9	39.7	60.3
Kinsman	4.4	24.0	28.4	71.6
Central–East	9.2	24.2	33.4	66.6
Central	4.0	15.5	19.5	80.5
Central–West	8.0	19.9	27.9	72.1
City Total	13.7	40.0	53.7	46.3
Suburbs	31.6	44.5	76.1	23.9
County Total	19.7	41.5	61.2	38.8

HOMICIDE IN AN URBAN COMMUNITY 131

smaller percentage of professionals and managers. One marked deviation, that of the University area, is to be explained, as are other "abnormalities" of that area, by the atypicality and heterogeneity of its population which includes many students and employees of the University and similar institutions in the vicinity. In both graphs, the percentages for city, county, and suburbs are presented as standards of comparison.

Table 44 adds to the picture the percentage of workers in class B (middle status) and the total for classes A and B.

Finally, for comparison, the five areas with the greatest proportion of professionals and managers are:

TABLE 45

Area	*A* *Per Cent of* *Professional* *and Managers*	*B* *Per Cent* *Clerical,* *Sales and* *Crafts*	*Total* *A and B*	*Per Cent* *Others*	*Homicide* *Rate*
Shaker-Beechwood	50.4	31.8	82.2	17.8	0.5
Cleveland-University Heights	45.7	40.8	86.5	13.5	0.7
West Shore	42.6	41.7	84.3	15.7	0.7
Chagrin Valley	36.4	35.8	72.2	27.8	1.6
South Euclid-Lyndhurst	33.0	45.4	78.4	21.6	0.5

It is interesting, but not significant, that none of the seven areas with homicide rates of zero are among the seven with the highest proportion of professionals. These seven areas with zero rates do rank, for the most part, however, among the highest third.

DENSITY OF POPULATION: GREATER DENSITY SETS THE STAGE FOR HOMICIDE!

Some areas are much more densely populated than others. Density is measured in persons per net acre, that is the ratio of population to net acres. "Net acres" means the area available for living space. The density of the social planning areas ranges from

132   *HOMICIDE IN AN URBAN COMMUNITY*

a minimum of 0.30 (Chagrin Valley) to a maximum of 65.26 (Central—West). The densest area is more than 200 times as dense as the most sparsely populated area. Generally the suburbs are less dense than the city areas, having as a whole a density of 1.91 compared to the city's 29.24.

The problem is to determine whether high density is associated with a high homicide rate. One would think that a more crowded area would suffer from various social problems, one of which would be homicide. Moreover, one would suppose that crowded conditions would bring people into greater and more frequent contact with increased likelihood of tensions developing and with an increased opportunity for violence. A glance at Graph 26 bears out this general idea.

The three most homicidal areas have the highest densities. But the correlation is far from perfect, as shown by the up-and-down pattern of the graph line. The sparsest areas in the county have

TABLE 46

TABULAR SUMMARY OF GRAPH 26: DENSITY OF POPULATION

Area	Density in Persons per Net Acre
West Side	30.21
Clark-Fulton	33.55
Norwood	51.24
University	34.74
Mount Pleasant	31.37
Glenville	33.47
Hough	58.03
North Broadway	30.82
Downtown	50.32
Goodrich	33.47
Kinsman	46.46
Central—East	58.53
Central	63.05
Central—West	65.26
City	29.24
Suburbs	1.91
County	4.98

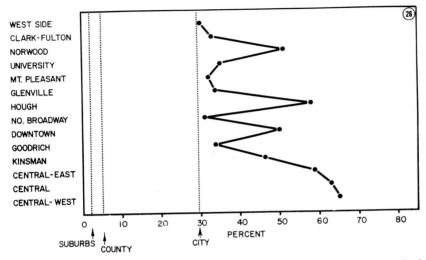

Graph 26. Density of the 14 Areas with the Highest Homicide Rate (ranked from the lowest to the highest). Density in Persons per Net Acre.

quite low homicide rates. But they are all suburban areas. Yet the same is true if the City of Cleveland alone is analyzed. The five sparse areas in the city are listed below with their homicide rates.

Clearly, then, at the extremes of high and low density, density itself is an important index associated with homicide. The densest areas have the highest rate; the least dense areas among the lowest rates. But the pattern between the extremes is so irregular and full of variations that it is difficult to draw conclusions.

TABLE 47

Area	Density	Homicide Rate
Riverside	9.09	0
Lee-Miles	9.39	1.9
Puritas-Bellaire	10.26	1.0
South Brooklyn	17.43	1.6
South Collinwood	21.37	0.5

Photograph 12. This area of highest population density has the highest homicide rate.

OVERCROWDED HOUSING:[5] HIGH HOMICIDE RATE AND OVERCROWDED HOUSING FORM PERFECT CORRELATION!

The number of persons who occupy the dwelling unit is apparently a more reliable index than the number of persons who occupy the total livable area. The progression on the graph from the West Side through a dozen intermediate areas to Central–West, is one of almost perfect correlation between high homicide rate and overcrowded housing. There are three noteworthy deviations: University and Downtown, the two atypical areas, which tend to crowded dwellings, and Central–East, which is strikingly lower than the surrounding areas on the graph.

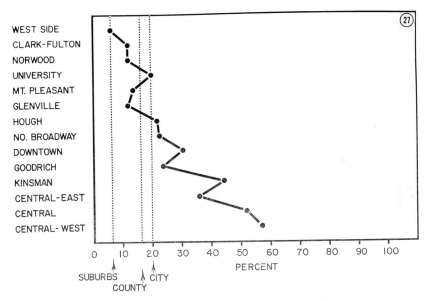

Graph 27. Percentage of Overcrowded Housing.

---

[5] Overcrowded housing is defined as the percentage of dwelling units having more than 1.01 persons per room to total occupied dwelling units.

Photograph 13. Overcrowded housing is a social factor in the highest homcide area.

HOMICIDE IN AN URBAN COMMUNITY

Photograph 14. Four persons in one bed are not conducive to peaceful living.

TABLE 48
TABULAR SUMMARY OF GRAPH 27: PERCENTAGE OF OVERCROWDED HOUSING

Area	Percent
West Side	5.26
Clark-Fulton	7.40
Norwood	7.33
University	10.18
Mt. Pleasant	7.56
Glenville	7.17
Hough	11.31
North Broadway	12.13
Downtown	15.18
Goodrich	13.25
Kinsman	22.15
Central—East	17.07
Central	25.66
Central—West	27.70
City Total	10.12
Suburban Total	4.81
County Total	8.29

AGE OF DWELLINGS AND SUBSTANDARD HOUSING:[6] FORMER INSIGNIFICANT, LATTER VERY SIGNIFICANT FACTOR IN HOMICIDE AREAS!

The age of the housing, on the other hand, apparently has little significance to homicide. Except for the fact that thirteen of the fourteen areas with the highest rate of homicide have a larger proportion of pre-1920 housing than the city as a whole, Graph 28 shows no relationship between the two factors. Central—West has a homicide rate sixteen times as great as the West Side; yet it has less "ancient" housing.

The percentage of dwelling units which are substandard is of greater importance. With the marked exception of the Downtown area, Graph 29 shows as a general pattern that the more substandard housing an area has, the higher is the homicide rate. Mount Pleasant and Glenville have very little substandard housing and are, therefore, somewhat unusual. But the six most homi-

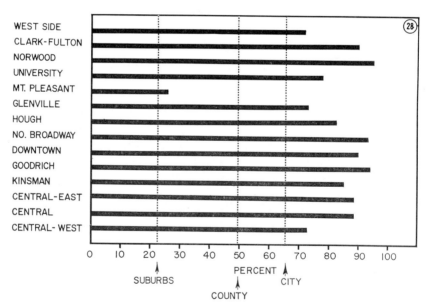

Graph 28. Percentage of Dwellings Built Before 1920.

---

[6]Substandard dwelling units include those which are dilapidated or without private bath.

TABLE 49

Tabular Summary of Graph 28: Percentage of Dwellings Built before 1920

Area	Percent
West Side	72.80
Clark-Fulton	90.55
Norwood	95.44
University	78.12
Mt. Pleasant	25.74
Glenville	73.38
Hough	83.33
North Broadway	93.43
Downtown	89.84
Goodrich	94.53
Kinsman	84.58
Central—East	92.25
Central	92.09
Central—West	69.14
City Total	65.05
Suburban Total	23.25
County Total	50.48

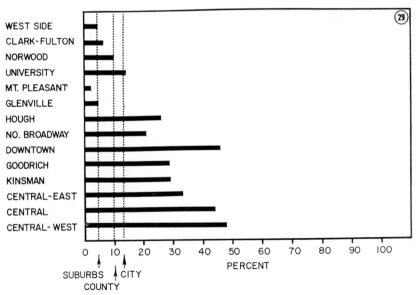

Graph 29. Percentage of Substandard Housing.

140 *HOMICIDE IN AN URBAN COMMUNITY*

TABLE 50

TABULAR SUMMARY OF GRAPH 29: PERCENTAGE OF SUBSTANDARD HOUSING

Area	Percent
West Side	3.95
Clark-Fulton	7.13
Norwood	10.64
University	14.16
Mt. Pleasant	2.39
Glenville	4.83
Hough	26.37
North Broadway	21.18
Downtown	45.76
Goodrich	28.80
Kinsman	28.90
Central—East	32.35
Central	43.65
Central—West	46.93
City Total	13.74
Suburban Total	4.02
County Total	10.36

cidal areas (omitting Downtown) rank as the six with the highest proportion of substandard housing.

OWNER-OCCUPIED DWELLING UNITS: OWNER-OCCUPIED DWELLINGS TEND TO PRODUCE LESS HOMICIDE!

It speaks something of the comparative social status of two areas that in one, less than 8% of the dwelling units are occupied by their owners and in the other, more than 55% are so occupied. The apparent significance of these figures is enhanced when one realizes that both of these areas are among the fourteen most homicidal areas. But a careful study of the graph will dispel the appearance of significance. The variations among these fourteen areas cannot be rationalized or explained away. Apparently there is only a loose association of this index with homicide, yet it is not to be entirely ignored.

Photograph 15. Over-age dwellings do not mean high homicide areas. This home, nearly three-quarters of a century old, has been well maintained and modernized. It is located in a very low homicide area where 95% of the housing is over 40 years old.

Photograph 16. The correlation between substandard housing and homicide rate is nearly perfect—the lower the housing standards the higher the homicide rate.

142   HOMICIDE IN AN URBAN COMMUNITY

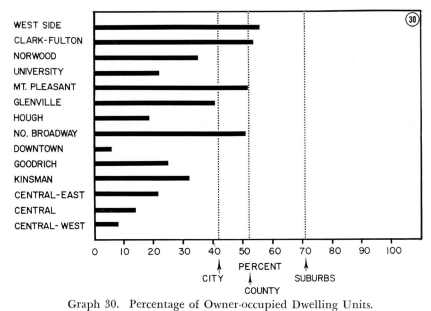

Graph 30. Percentage of Owner-occupied Dwelling Units.

TABLE 51
TABULAR SUMMARY OF GRAPH 30: PERCENTAGE OF OWNER-OCCUPIED DWELLING UNITS

Area	Percent
West Side	56.60
Clark-Fulton	54.27
Norwood	34.87
University	21.97
Mt. Pleasant	51.93
Glenville	40.79
Hough	19.14
North Broadway	51.04
Downtown	7.64
Goodrich	24.97
Kinsman	32.04
Central—East	21.98
Central	13.54
Central—West	7.68
City Total	42.65
Suburban Total	70.89
County Total	52.38

MARRIED COUPLES WITHOUT THEIR OWN HOUSEHOLD: A SIGNIFICANT FACTOR IN HOMICIDE AREAS!

A far more significant index is that of the percentage of married couples who do not have their own household. A moment's reflection will show the social significance of this index. The social problems attributable to a high percentage of married couples without their own household are obvious. With the exception of the atypical Downtown area, the only three areas in which 20% or more of married couples are in this position are the three areas which constitute the highest homicide areas.

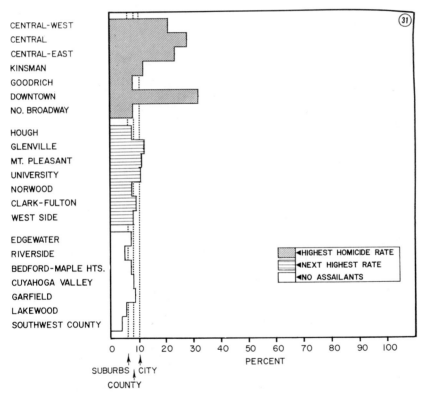

Graph 31. Percentage of Married Couples without Own Household.

Photograph 17. All these married couples do not own their own household. Eighteen persons in five families live on the second floor sharing one kitchen and one bath. Another important factor in high homicide areas.

HOMICIDE IN AN URBAN COMMUNITY

TABLE 52

TABULAR SUMMARY OF GRAPH 31: PERCENTAGE OF MARRIED COUPLES
WITHOUT OWN HOUSEHOLD

Area	Percent
Central—West	20.5
Central	28.6
Central—East	23.0
Kinsman	12.7
Goodrich	8.2
Downtown	32.1
North Broadway	8.2
Hough	7.1
Glenville	12.9
Mt. Pleasant	11.1
University	11.2
Norwood	7.9
Clark-Fulton	8.4
West Side	8.3
Edgewater	7.7
Riverside	5.0
Bedford-Maple Heights	7.2
Cuyahoga Valley	8.1
Garfield	9.1
Lakewood	5.9
Southwest County	4.7
City of Cleveland	10.1
Suburbs	6.3
Cuyahoga County	8.7

AID FOR THE AGED: A GOOD INDICATOR OF HOMICIDAL NEIGHBORHOODS!

The proportion of aged persons who receive aid from public funds is a double-indicator of the economic condition of an area. In the first place, the fact that a large percentage receive such aid would seem to show that the elderly segment of the population is in large measure without adequate means to be self-sufficient. In the second place, it would tend to indicate that the adult popula-

Photograph 18. This area with the greatest owner-occupied dwellings and married couples owning their own homes experienced no homicides in the entire seven year period. Population density is low; 9.09 persons per net acre.

tion in general, the heads of families whose parents constitute the aged, are not in a position to support their parents.

Graph 32 and Table 53 show the fairly close association between a high proportion of aid recipients and a high rate of homicide. Most striking is the high relative position of the three areas which have the highest homicide rates.

It will be noted that the data on this and several of the following graphs are for 1953, rather than 1950. Since this is the last year of the homicide study, rather than its mid-year, the correlations are somewhat less reliable. This should not, however, in most cases, detract materially from the essential validity of what the graphs seem to portray.

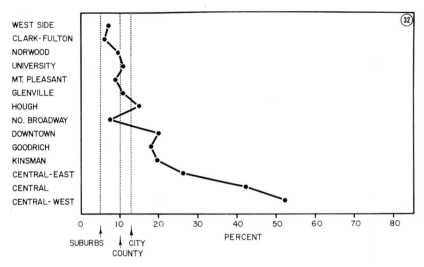

Graph 32. Aid for the Aged Recipients. Per Cent of Population 65 Years and Over (1953).

TABLE 53

Tabular Summary of Graph 32: Aid for the Aged Recipients. Per Cent of Population 65 Years and Over (1953)

Area	Percentage
West Side	7.22
Clark-Fulton	6.14
Norwood	9.46
University	10.42
Mt. Pleasant	8.94
Glenville	10.60
Hough	15.81
North Broadway	7.76
Downtown	20.29
Goodrich	18.34
Kinsman	19.66
Central—East	26.58
Central	41.75
Central—West	51.77
City Total	12.50
Suburbs Total	4.96
County Total	9.94

PUBLIC ASSISTANCE CASES: ANOTHER GOOD BAROMETER OF HOMICIDAL PRESSURE!

With the exception of the atypical Downtown area, this correlation seems even more definite than in the case of Aid for the Aged. No comment is necessary, except to reiterate the caution necessitated by the fact that the data are for 1953.

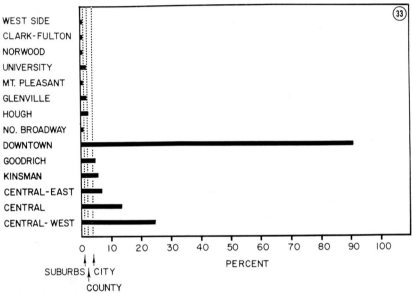

Graph 33. Public Assistance Cases. Rate per 100 Occupied Family Units (1953).

CHILDREN ACCEPTED FOR SERVICE: NO RELATIONSHIP TO THE HOMICIDAL RATE OF A NEIGHBORHOOD!

Graph 34 shows the almost total absence of a meaningful relationship between homicide and the social indicator comprised by the rate at which children are accepted for service. As *possible* explanations for this somewhat surprising fact, the following are offered:

1) The youth services whose activities are covered by the data may not furnish a comprehensive index of the true total picture.

HOMICIDE IN AN URBAN COMMUNITY

TABLE 54

TABULAR SUMMARY OF GRAPH 33: PUBLIC ASSISTANCE CASES.[7]
RATE PER ONE HUNDRED OCCUPIED UNITS

Area	Rate
West Side	0.80
Clark-Fulton	0.45
Norwood	1.01
University	2.03
Mt. Pleasant	1.21
Glenville	1.95
Hough	2.30
North Broadway	1.42
Downtown	81.82
Goodrich	4.31
Kinsman	6.42
Central—East	7.88
Central	15.78
Central—West	25.26
City of Cleveland	3.49
Suburbs	0.37
Cuyahoga County	2.26

2) Although the poorer neighborhoods will obviously register a higher rate than the wealthier neighborhoods, factors other than wealth may play a role. For example, it is possible that families with less education may be less prone to send their children to the existing services than families with equal need which are somewhat better educated.

In any event, the by-now familiar correlation pattern is not present in this instance.

---

[7]Includes families receiving aid for dependent children, aid for the disabled, Cuyahoga County Welfare Department relief cases and relief cases of Cleveland and all suburbs.

150   HOMICIDE IN AN URBAN COMMUNITY

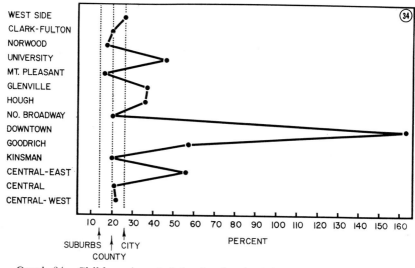

Graph 34. Children Accepted for Service—by Three Private Child-placing Agencies. Rate per 10,000 Children (1953).

TABLE 55

TABULAR SUMMARY OF GRAPH 34: CHILDREN ACCEPTED FOR SERVICE BY THREE PRIVATE CHILD-PLACING AGENCIES, 1953.[8] RATE PER 10,000 CHILDREN

Area	Rate
West Side	26.02
Clark-Fulton	20.36
Norwood	17.21
University	45.77
Mt. Pleasant	16.51
Glenville	37.03
Hough	35.75
North Broadway	21.19
Downtown	163.93
Goodrich	57.56
Kinsman	20.03
Central—East	55.98
Central	21.29
Central—West	23.11
Cleveland Total	26.06
Suburban Total	13.57
County Total	21.58

[8]Includes children accepted for service during 1953 by the Catholic Charities Bureau, Children's Services and the Jewish Children's Bureau.

ILLEGITIMATE BIRTHRATE: WHEN EXTREMELY HIGH A GOOD INDICATOR OF A HIGH HOMICIDE RATE!

The four most homicidal areas had remarkably higher illegitimate birthrates than the areas with relatively lower rates of homicide. On the other hand, the differences between such areas as Norwood, Clark-Fulton, and the West Side and such areas as Edgewater, Riverside, and Bedford-Maple Heights were small and the progression irregular. Apparently the illegitimate birthrate is a significant index only when it is extremely high.

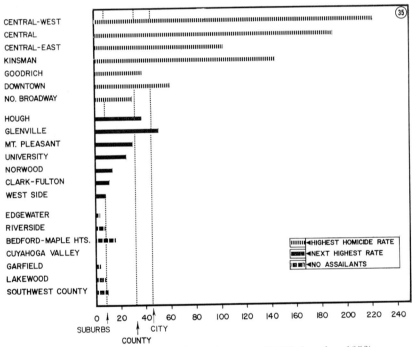

Graph 35. Illegitimate Birthrate (rate per 10,000 females, 1953).

TABLE 56

TABULAR SUMMARY OF GRAPH 35: ILLEGITIMATE BIRTHRATE.
RATE PER 10,000 FEMALES (1953)

Area	Rate
Central—West	222.3
Central	189.9
Central—East	103.4
Kinsman	143.9
Goodrich	38.9
Downtown	60.6
North Broadway	31.4
Hough	37.5
Glenville	51.0
Mt. Pleasant	32.8
University	25.6
Norwood	14.0
Clark-Fulton	11.2
West Side	9.1
Edgewater	3.7
Riverside	8.5
Bedford-Maple Heights	16.5
Cuyahoga Valley	0.0
Garfield	4.7
Lakewood	8.6
Southwest County	9.8
City Total	45.3
Suburbs Total	8.8
County Total	33.3

JUVENILE DELINQUENCY; NEGLECT AND DEPENDENCE COMPLAINTS: GOOD HOMICIDE INDICATORS!

One would expect juvenile delinquency to be highly correlated with dependency and neglect, and both of these indices with homicide. Graphs 36 and 37, with their Tables 57 and 58, largely confirm this expectation. The areas of high homicide represent by far the greatest number of such complaints. The deviations from a perfect correlation should, however, be noted, as should the fact that the data are for 1953, the end year of the homicide study.

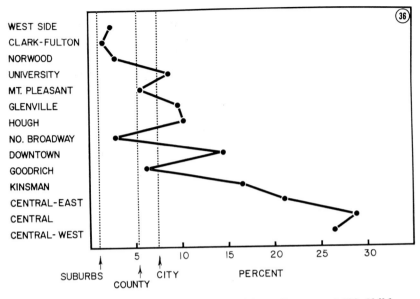

Graph 36. Neglect and Dependency Complaints. Rate per 1,000 Children Under 18 Years of Age (1953).

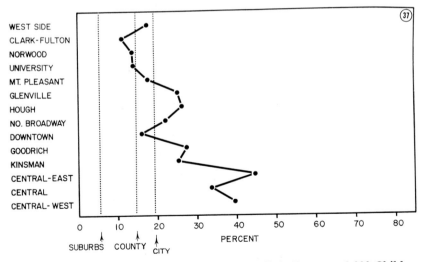

Graph 37. Juvenile Delinquency Complaints Filed. Rate per 1,000 Children 5 to 17 Years of Age (1953).

154   *HOMICIDE IN AN URBAN COMMUNITY*

TABLE 57

TABULAR SUMMARY OF GRAPH 36: NEGLECT AND DEPENDENCY COMPLAINTS.
RATE PER 1,000 CHILDREN UNDER 18 YEARS OF AGE (1953)[9]

Area	Rate
West Side	2.05
Clark-Fulton	1.45
Norwood	2.72
University	8.01
Mount Pleasant	5.57
Glenville	9.33
Hough	10.13
North Broadway	2.64
Downtown	14.21
Goodrich	6.37
Kinsman	16.03
Central—East	20.87
Central	28.67
Central—West	26.10
Cleveland Total	7.39
Suburbs Total	1.12
County Total	5.14

It should also be borne in mind that some suburban areas are lax in the matter of reporting cases of delinquency to the Juvenile Court, preferring to handle the matter themselves. This reduces the number of cases shown for such areas.

---

[9]The "neglect" complaints include unofficial and official complaints. The "dependency" complaints include official cases only.

TABLE 58

TABULAR SUMMARY OF GRAPH 37: JUVENILE DELINQUENCY COMPLAINTS FILED.[10]
RATE PER 1,000 CHILDREN 5 TO 17 YEARS OF AGE (1953)

Area	Rate
West Side	17.16
Clark-Fulton	11.24
Norwood	13.05
University	13.45
Mount Pleasant	17.47
Glenville	25.40
Hough	26.28
North Broadway	22.42
Downtown	16.10
Goodrich	27.13
Kinsman	25.33
Central—East	42.31
Central	33.35
Central—West	39.55
Cleveland Total	19.32
Suburbs Total	5.47
County Total	14.24

TUBERCULOSIS AND INFANT MORTALITY: THE FORMER IS A BETTER GUIDE THAN THE LATTER TO HOMICIDAL AREAS!

The Downtown area excepted, the progression from the lower to higher rates of tuberculosis coincides fairly closely with the progression in homicide rates. The infant mortality rate shows no such regularity. In both cases, however, the three most homicidal areas are among those with the highest rates in these two health traits.

---

[10]Includes all official and unofficial complaints filed except traffic complaints.

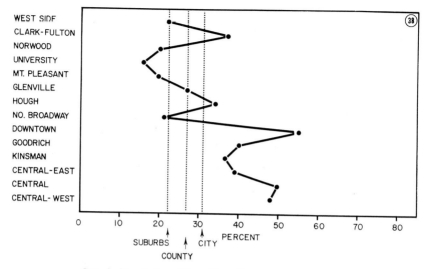

Graph 38. Infant Mortality. Rate per 1,000 (1953).

TABLE 59

TABULAR SUMMARY OF GRAPH 38: INFANT MORTALITY RATE PER 1,000 (1953)

Area	Rate
West Side	21.9
Clark-Fulton	36.9
Norwood	20.4
University	15.9
Mount Pleasant	19.8
Glenville	27.8
Hough	34.7
North Broadway	21.4
Downtown	55.0
Goodrich	40.4
Kinsman	36.8
Central—East	38.7
Central	49.8
Central—West	48.3
City Total	31.0
Suburbs Total	22.3
County Total	27.7

HOMICIDE IN AN URBAN COMMUNITY 157

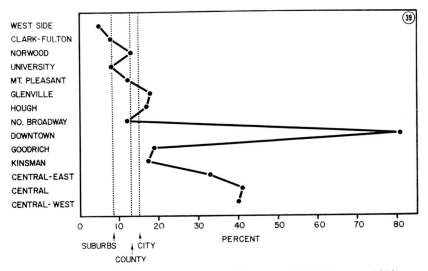

Graph 39. Tuberculosis: New Cases. Rate per 10,000 Persons (1953).

TABLE 60

TABULAR SUMMARY OF GRAPH 39: TUBERCULOSIS: NEW CASES.
RATE PER 10,000 PERSONS (1953)

Area	Rate
West Side	4.95
Clark-Fulton	8.17
Norwood	13.18
University	8.75
Mount Pleasant	12.29
Glenville	18.31
Hough	17.20
North Broadway	11.46
Downtown	81.24
Goodrich	19.14
Kinsman	17.61
Central–East	32.89
Central	41.21
Central–West	40.38
Cleveland Total	15.18
Suburbs Total	8.72
County Total	12.98

Chapter III

THE HOMICIDE RATE AND OTHER SOCIAL INDICATORS

In the study "Measuring Leisure Time Needs," a series of indices of area characteristics and social needs were produced. Each index is composed of a number of factors. In computing a given index an effort was made to weigh the characteristics which went to make it up in such a manner as to produce the most reliable possible index. Table 61 lists the indices and the component factors which comprise them.

After the indices were computed for all 41[11] social planning areas, the areas were then ranked according to the magnitude of each index.

For the purpose of the homicide study the rank of the most homicidal areas on each of these indices should be determined. This correlation will provide a generalization perhaps more useful than the particularized correlation graphs presented earlier.

PROCEDURE

For each of the nine indices two procedures were used:
1) The thirteen areas with the highest rate of homicide were listed on the X-axis, in descending order of homicide rate.[12] Then their ranks on the given social index were plotted. The resulting graph is indicative of the degree of relationship or association (not necessarily causal) between the trait or traits involved in the index and the incidence of homicide. It was not considered necessary to chart all the social planning areas, for the top thirteen cover a wide span of

---

[11]In this computation the Downtown area was excluded because of its atypicality.
[12]The Downtown area was excluded because of its omission in the index rankings.

HOMICIDE IN AN URBAN COMMUNITY

TABLE 61

Index	Component Factors
1. Socio-Economic Status	Median family income, median school grade completed, and rate (percent) of managerial and professional workers to total employed persons.
2. Undesirable Neighborhood Conditions	Converted and miscellaneous dwelling units, flats over stores, age of dwellings, and substandard housing. ("Substandard housing" consists of dwelling units which are dilapidated or which lack private bath.)
3. Financial Dependency	Aid for the Aged and public relief.
4. Space	Population density and overcrowded housing.
5. Crowded Housing Conditions	Overcrowded housing and the number of married couples without their own households.
6. Stability of Population	Population movement within the county (1949-1950), population movement into the county (1949-1950), percentage of owner-occupied dwelling units, percentage of converted and miscellaneous dwelling units.
7. Social Maladjustment	Juvenile delinquency, child neglect and dependency, private agency child-placing and illegitimate birthrate.
8. Family and Individual Adjustment Problems	Family agency cases, private youth agency cases.
9. Ill Health	New tuberculosis cases, and infant mortality.

homicide rate (4.2 to 72.2); indeed they cover nearly the entire range of rates.

2) In order, nevertheless, to study the relationship between homicide and other social indicators, in the more favored areas (high social status—low homicide rate) another less precise device was employed. It will be recalled that the social

160   *HOMICIDE IN AN URBAN COMMUNITY*

planning areas were earlier arranged in five groups according to homicide rate. Then the constituent areas in each quintile were ranked on the various social indices and the average rank of the area in that quintile was computed. This furnishes a comparison in large groups among the low-homicide and high-homicide areas. The Downtown area, again, was omitted.

It will be noted in studying these graphs and tables that the difference in average rank is the greatest between the first quintile (highest homicide rate) and the second. This accords with what was noted earlier, namely, that the graph of homicide is quite skewed toward the upper end and that the rate in the most homicidal areas is considerably higher than that in the next highest. The difference between these homicide rates is much greater than that between the next highest and the very lowest. Therefore it is not surprising that the differences in average rank on the social indices are less among the four less homicidal quintiles than between the first and the others. In fact, the fifth quintile sometimes ranks higher in certain indices of social need than the fourth quintile. This is not unusual if one notes the slightness of the difference in homicide rates between those two quintiles. The fifth quintile consists of those areas from which there came *no assailants*. The four quintile consists of areas from which there came *almost no assailants*. The difference between a homicide rate of zero and one of 0.4 is, to all practical intents, negligible, and the fact that a given area is in one quintile rather than the other is largely fortuitous. It would probably be better to compute a single average rank for the fourth and fifth quintiles, but it was thought desirable to keep the quintiles at least approximately equal in the number of areas included.

To give point to the fact that only the thirteen most homicidal areas are graphed, a broken line has been entered for comparison. It represents the average rank of the fifth homicide quintile, *i.e.* the areas with a zero rate of homicide. The rank of the 13 highest homicide areas is consistently above this average. But that average is of limited significance, for—as will be seen—the average rank of the *fourth* quintile is often lower. Moreover, when only a few

HOMICIDE IN AN URBAN COMMUNITY

areas are involved (as is the case in each quintile) a single acutely deviating area, *e.g.* one which ranks unusually high or low on a given trait, will markedly affect the average.

SOCIO-ECONOMIC STATUS

The lower the socio-economic status of an area, the higher is its homicide rate. The exception is the University area, which, despite a relatively high socio-economic status, has a substantial homicide rate.

TABLE 62

AVERAGE RANK BY HOMICIDE QUINTILES

Homicide Quintile	Average Rank in Socio-Economic Status (highest rank is lowest status)
1 (highest rate)	36.85
2	24.5
3	19.12
4	13.0
5 (lowest rate)	12.57

The progression in average rank is as expected. And, also as expected, the interval between the average ranks is greatest in the case of the first and second quintiles.

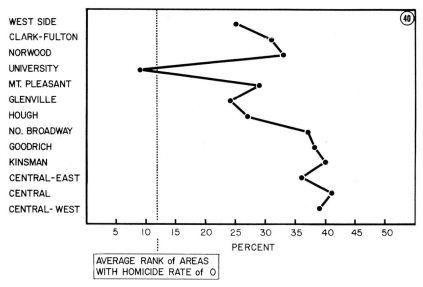

Graph 40. Index of Socio-Economic Status—13 Areas Ranked from Highest Status to Lowest. (*Rank in Homicide Rate.)

TABLE 63

Tabular Summary of Graph 40: Ranking of 13 Areas[13] as to Socio-Economic Status[14]

Area	Homicide Rate Rank[15]	Rank (out of 41)
West Side	29	25
Clark-Fulton	30	31
Norwood	31	33
University	32	9
Mount Pleasant	33	29
Glenville	34	24
Hough	35	27
North Broadway	36	37
Goodrich	37	38
Kinsman	38	40
Central—East	39	36
Central	40	41
Central—West	41	39

[13] The thirteen areas, excluding Downtown, which had the highest rate of homicide.
[14] Ranked from highest status to lowest.
[15] Ranked from the lowest to the highest rate among the highest thirteen.

UNDESIRABLE NEIGHBORHOOD CONDITIONS

Again, with a single exception, the progression from lower to higher rate of homicide accompanies rather regularly the progression upward on the scale of undesirability of neighborhood conditions.

TABLE 64

Average Rank by Homicide Quintiles

Homicide Quintile	Rank in Undesirable Neighborhood Condition (highest rank is least desirable)
1 (highest rate)	37.14
2	24.6
3	15.5
4	14.22
5 (lowest rate)	14.71

The first interval is again the largest.

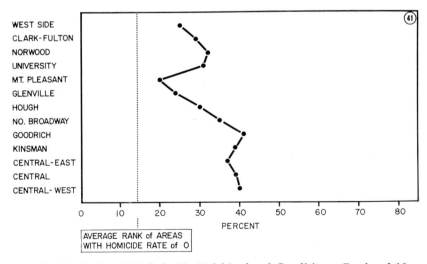

Graph 41. Index of Undesirable Neighborhood Conditions. Ranks of 13 Areas. Ranked from Least to Most Undesirable.

164   *HOMICIDE IN AN URBAN COMMUNITY*

TABLE 65

Tabular Summary of Graph 41: Ranking of 13 Areas[16] as to Undesirable Neighborhood Conditions[17]

Area	Homicide Rate Rank[18]	Rank (out of 41)
West Side	29	25
Clark-Fulton	30	29
Norwood	31	32
University	32	31
Mount Pleasant	33	20
Glenville	34	24
Hough	35	30
North Broadway	36	35
Goodrich	37	41
Kinsman	38	38
Central—East	39	37
Central	40	39
Central—West	41	40

FINANCIAL DEPENDENCY

With some marked deviations, Graph 42 and Table 67 show quite clearly the association of financial dependency and homicide.

This distribution of quintile averages in Table 66 points up the fact that the differences among areas in the fourth quintile as a group and those in the fifth (zero rate of homicide) are not significant. Indeed, the lowest quintile is more dependent financially than is the fourth.

TABLE 66

Average Rank by Homicide Quintiles

Homicide Quintile	Average Rank in Financial Dependency (highest rank is greatest dependency)
1 (highest rate)	37.0
2	23.2
3	19.0
4	12.66
5 (lowest rate)	15.14

[16]The thirteen areas, excluding Downtown, which had the highest rate of homicide.

[17]Ranked from least to most undesirable.

[18]Ranked from the lowest to the highest rate among the highest thirteen.

HOMICIDE IN AN URBAN COMMUNITY 165

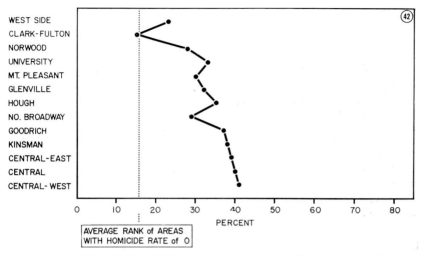

Graph 42. Index of Financial Dependency. Ranks of 13 Areas. Ranked from Least to Greatest Dependency. (*Rank in Homicide Rate.)

TABLE 67

TABULAR SUMMARY OF GRAPH 42: RANKING OF 13 AREAS[19] AS TO FINANCIAL DEPENDENCY[20]

Area	Homicidal Rate Rank[21]	Rank (out of 41)
West Side	29	23
Clark-Fulton	30	15
Norwood	31	28
University	32	33
Mount Pleasant	33	30
Glenville	34	32
Hough	35	35
North Broadway	36	29
Goodrich	37	37
Kinsman	38	38
Central—East	39	39
Central	40	40
Central—West	41	41

[19] The thirteen areas, excluding Downtown, which had the highest homicide rate.
[20] Ranked from least to greatest dependency.
[21] Ranked from lowest to highest rate among the highest thirteen.

SPACE

The areas in which people have the least space in which to live are the highest in homicide. With some irregularity, the course of Graph 43, Tables 68 and 69 from the less homicidal to the more homicidal areas, is upward.

These should be compared with crowded housing conditions.

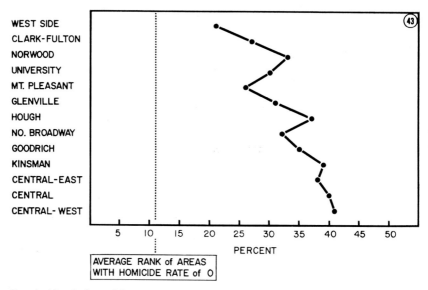

Graph 43. Index of Space. Ranks of 13 Areas (ranked from greatest to least space).

TABLE 68

AVERAGE RANK BY HOMICIDE QUINTILES

Homicide Quintile	Average Rank in Space (the higher the number, the less space)
1 (highest rate)	37.42
2	26.1
3	18.25
4	12.77
5 (lowest rate)	11.0

HOMICIDE IN AN URBAN COMMUNITY

TABLE 69

TABULAR SUMMARY OF GRAPH 43: RANKING OF 13 AREAS[22] AS TO SPACE[23]

Area	Homicide Rate Rank[24]	Rank (out of 41)
West Side	29	21
Clark-Fulton	30	27
Norwood	31	33
University	32	30
Mount Pleasant	33	26
Glenville	34	31
Hough	35	37
North Broadway	36	32
Goodrich	37	35
Kinsman	38	39
Central—East	39	38
Central	40	40
Central—West	41	41

CROWDED HOUSING CONDITIONS

Graph 44 with Tables 70 and 71 speaks for itself.

The possible explanations for the relative average ranks of the fourth and fifth quintiles have been commented on previously.

TABLE 70

AVERAGE RANK BY HOMICIDE QUINTILES

Homicide Quintile	Rank in Crowded Housing Condition (the higher the rank, the greater the crowding)
1 (highest rate)	37.42
2	24.75
3	17.93
4	10.88
5 (lowest rate)	15.71

[22]The thirteen areas, excluding Downtown, which had the highest rate of homicide.

[23]Ranked from greatest to least space.

[24]Ranked from the lowest to the highest rate among the highest thirteen.

Photograph 19. The space age is upon us. In local communities space is a vital element related to the homicide rate. Areas where people have the least space in which to live represent the highest homicide areas. Population density in this highest homicide area is 65.26 persons per net acre. Perhaps man should learn to handle earth space better, before he becomes so concerned with moon space.

HOMICIDE IN AN URBAN COMMUNITY 169

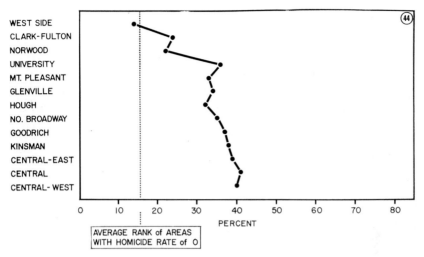

Graph 44. Index of Crowded Housing Conditions. Ranks of 13 Areas (ranked from least crowded to most crowded).

TABLE 71

Tabular Summary of Graph 44: Ranking of 13 Areas[25] as to Crowded Housing Conditions[26]

Area	Homicide Rate Rank[27]	Rank (out of 41)
West Side	29	14
Clark-Fulton	30	24
Norwood	31	22
University	32	36
Mount Pleasant	33	33
Glenville	34	34
Hough	35	32
North Broadway	36	35
Goodrich	37	37
Kinsman	38	38
Central—East	39	39
Central	40	41
Central—West	41	40

[25] The thirteen areas, excluding Downtown, which had the highest rate of homicide.
[26] Ranked from least crowded to most crowded.
[27] Ranked from the lowest to the highest rate among the highest thirteen.

POPULATION STABILITY

This index is somewhat misleading. Because of the component factors, two types of areas will tend to show a *high instability*. Very poor areas and very new areas. Graph 45, with the ever-present deviations, nonetheless presents some indication that the homicidal areas have, relative to most areas, much movement of population.

These graphs and tables apparently should only be interpreted as stating something about the most unstable areas. Beyond that, the fluctuation of variables is too great.

TABLE 72

AVERAGE RANK BY HOMICIDE QUINTILES

Homicide Quintile	Average Rank in Population Stability (the higher the rank the less the stability)
1 (highest rate)	37.14
2	22.1
3	12.75
4	18.55
5 (lowest rate)	15.85

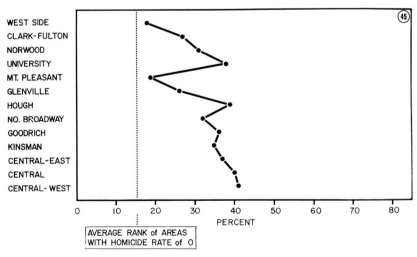

Graph 45. Index of Population Stability. Ranks of 13 Areas (ranked from greatest to least stability).

HOMICIDE IN AN URBAN COMMUNITY

171

TABLE 73

TABULAR SUMMARY OF GRAPH 45: RANKING OF 13 AREAS[28] AS TO
POPULATION STABILITY[29]

Area	Homicide Rate Rank[30]	Rank (out of 41)
West Side	29	18
Clark-Fulton	30	27
Norwood	31	31
University	32	38
Mount Pleasant	33	19
Glenville	34	26
Hough	35	39
North Broadway	36	32
Goodrich	37	36
Kinsman	38	35
Central—East	39	37
Central	40	40
Central—West	41	41

SOCIAL MALADJUSTMENT

The rather high correlation between homicide and social maladjustment is not surprising. A thesis of this study has been that
homicide is in itself a reflection of social maladjustment.

TABLE 74

AVERAGE RANK BY HOMICIDE QUINTILES

Homicide Quintile	Average Rank in Social Maladjustment (the higher the rank the greater the maladjustment)
1 (highest rate)	37.14
2	25.1
3	19.75
4	11.44
5 (lowest rate)	12.71

[28]The thirteen areas, excluding Downtown, which had the highest rate of
homicide.

[29]Ranked from greatest to least stability.

[30]Ranked from the lowest to the highest rate among the highest thirteen.

172   HOMICIDE IN AN URBAN COMMUNITY

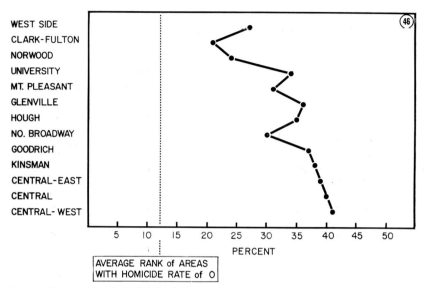

Graph 46. Index of Social Maladjustment. Ranks of 13 Areas (ranked from least to greatest maladjustment).

TABLE 75

Tabular Summary of Graph 46: Ranking of 13 Areas[31] as to Social Maladjustment[32]

Area	Homicide Rate Rank[33]	Rank (out of 41)
West Side	29	27
Clark-Fulton	30	21
Norwood	31	24
University	32	34
Mount Pleasant	33	31
Glenville	34	36
Hough	35	35
North Broadway	36	30
Goodrich	37	37
Kinsman	38	38
Central—East	39	39
Central	40	40
Central—West	41	41

[31] The thirteen areas, excluding Downtown, which had the highest rate of homicide.
[32] Ranked from least to greatest maladjustment.
[33] Ranked from the lowest to the highest rate among the highest thirteen.

FAMILY AND INDIVIDUAL ADJUSTMENT

Except for the marked deviation of the North Broadway area, whose deviation on Graph 47 was also noticeable, these tables and graphs show a fair degree of correlation.

TABLE 76

Average Rank by Homicide Quintiles

Homicide Quintile	Average Rank in Family and Individual Adjustment (the higher the rank the greater the lack of adjustment)
1 (highest rate)	36.0
2	23.1
3	18.37
4	13.77
5 (lowest rate)	15.28

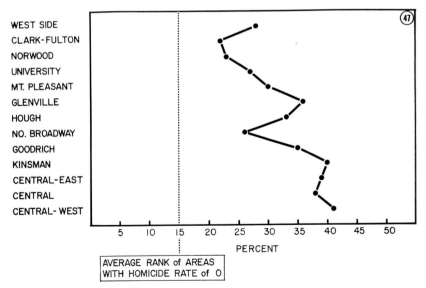

Graph 47. Index of Family and Individual Adjustment. Ranks of 13 Areas (ranked from least to greatest maladjustment).

TABLE 77

TABULAR SUMMARY OF GRAPH 47: RANKING OF 13 AREAS[34] AS TO FAMILY
AND INDIVIDUAL ADJUSTMENT[35]

Area	Homicide Rate Rank[36]	Rank (out of 41)
West Side	29	28
Clark-Fulton	30	22
Norwood	31	23
University	32	27
Mount Pleasant	33	30
Glenville	34	36
Hough	35	33
North Broadway	36	26
Goodrich	37	35
Kinsman	38	40
Central—East	39	39
Central	40	38
Central—West	41	41

ILL HEALTH

Ill health is most prevalent in the highest homicidal areas. The relatively high rate of tuberculosis and of infant mortality, two conditions which seem to reflect poverty and a poor physical environment, is proof. There are a few impressive departures from this general pattern, most notably the atypical University area.

---

[34]The thirteen areas, excluding Downtown, which had the highest rate of homicide.

[35]Ranked from least to greatest maladjustment.

[36]Ranked from the lowest to the highest rate among the highest thirteen.

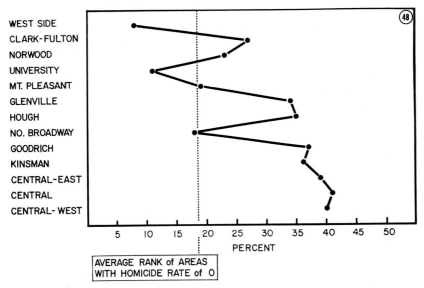

Graph 48. Index of Ill Health. Ranks of 13 Areas (ranked from least to greatest ill health).

TABLE 78

Average Rank by Homicide Quintiles

Homicide Quintile	Average Rank in Ill Health (the higher the rank, the greater the health problem)
1 (highest rate)	35.14
2	21.1
3	17.62
4	14.77
5 (lowest rate)	18.85

176　　　*HOMICIDE IN AN URBAN COMMUNITY*

TABLE 79

TABULAR SUMMARY OF GRAPH 48: RANKING OF 13 AREAS[37] AS TO ILL HEALTH[38]

Area	Homicide Rate Rank[39]	Rank (out of 41)
West Side	29	8
Clark-Fulton	30	27
Norwood	31	23
University	32	11
Mount Pleasant	33	19
Glenville	34	34
Hough	35	35
North Broadway	36	18
Goodrich	37	37
Kinsman	38	36
Central—East	39	39
Central	40	41
Central—West	41	40

---

[37]The thirteen areas, excluding Downtown, which had the highest rate of homicide.

[38]Ranked from least to greatest ill health.

[39]Ranked from lowest to highest rate among the highest thirteen.

Chapter IV

THE THREE HIGHEST HOMICIDE AREAS
COMPARED

The reader may have noticed that among the three contiguous areas with the highest rate of homicide, one is conspicuously lower than the other two.

TABLE 80

Area	Homicide Rate	No. of Assailants	No. Victims	No. Scenes
Central—West	72.2	204	193	235
Central	62.1	104	123	113
Central—East	24.1	63	74	60

The question arises whether this impressive gap between a rate of 24.1 in one area and rates of 62.1 and 72.2 in the other two is associated with any other significant differences. Upon tabulating the relative *ranks* of the three areas in the various social indicators, Central—East generally ranked immediately (sometimes a few ranks) below Central—West and Central. But ranking alone does not furnish an explanation for the great difference in homicide rate, for it does not reflect absolute differences. The pertinent facts about the three areas must be summarized. Perhaps some clue will appear.

Central—East has a larger proportion of Negroes than Central—West and a substantially lower homicide rate. *The percentage of Negroes in the population,* therefore, *is in itself* NOT *an index of the homicide rate.*

In economic statuses the differences are marked and suggestive. The median family income in Central—East is nearly $700 higher than in Central—West (more than 34% higher) and more than $300

177

TABLE 81

COMPARISON OF SOCIO-ECONOMIC INDICATORS IN THREE HIGHEST HOMICIDE AREAS

		Central-West Area	Central Area	Central-East Area
Percent of population which is Negro		77.2	95.3	81.7
Median Family income		$2051.50	$2369.50	$2703.00
Education:	Median grade completed	6.99	7.30	9.39
	Percent with no high school	63.5	61.6	46.9
Occupational distribution:	Percent managerial and professional	8.0	4.0	9.2
	Percent clerical, sales, and crafts	19.9	15.5	24.2
	Percent others, unskilled	72.1	80.5	66.6
Density: persons per net acre		65.26	63.05	58.53
Percent of overcrowded housing		27.70	25.66	17.07
Percent dwellings built before 1920		69.14	92.09	92.25
Percent substandard housing		46.93	43.65	32.35
Percent owner occupied dwelling units		7.68	13.54	21.98
Percent married couples without own household		20.5	28.6	23.0
Percent persons 65 + years receiving aid		51.77	41.75	26.58
Public assistance cases rate		25.26	15.78	7.88
Children accepted for service rate		23.11	21.29	55.98
Illegitimate birthrate		222.13	189.9	103.4
Neglect and dependency complaint rate		26.10	28.67	20.87
Juvenile delinquency complaint rate		39.55	33.35	42.31
Infant mortality rate		48.3	49.8	38.7
Tuberculosis rate		40.38	41.21	32.89

HOMICIDE IN AN URBAN COMMUNITY

higher than in Central. The percentage of older persons receiving aid for the aged is almost 50% less in Central—East than in Central—West. The rate of public assistance cases is 50% lower in Central—East than in Central and more than 75% lower than in Central—West. In short, Central—East has a much higher economic status than the other two areas.

One indicator seems to be awry. More than twice as large a proportion of children have been accepted for service in Central—East than in the other areas. But this harmonizes with what was stated in the comment on Graph 34 and Table 55—namely that it seems as if *this* index is not associated with the homicide rate, or at least that its correlation with financial need is offset by some other element—possibly the fact that the more highly educated families of those in economic straits are more likely to send their children to agencies than those with less education.

The data *re* education are equally revealing. The median grade completed in Central—East is nearly 2½ years above that in Central—West. Fifteen percent less persons entirely lack high school education in Central—East than in the other two areas. The percentage differences in high- and low-status occupational distribution are much smaller. But Central—East does have a larger proportion of managers, professionals, clerks, sales workers and craftsmen and a smaller proportion of unskilled workers than the other two areas.

The age of dwellings has already been determined to be an insignificant factor. In all the other housing indices (with one exception) Central-East is seen to be in a better position than the others. This is partly a concomitant of its economic position. It has a slightly lower density, 10% less overcrowded housing, and more than 10% less substandard housing. Much more impressive is the fact that the proportion of owner-occupied dwelling units in Central—East is 50% greater than in Central and 200% greater than in Central—West.

Although the rate of neglect and dependency complaints is lower in Central—East than in the other two areas, the juvenile delinquency rate is apparently higher. The only readily discernible explanation is that the data being for 1953 may reflect a progressive deterioration in the area, and that figures for 1949 or 1950 might

HOMICIDE IN AN URBAN COMMUNITY

have given different results. Even with this explanation, the situation is slightly anomalous.

The illegitimate birthrate is a dramatic example of the difference between Central—East and the other areas. It is nearly twice as high in Central and more than twice as high in Central—West.

A similar, though less spectacular situation is found by comparing the three areas as to infant mortality and the incidence of new cases of tuberculosis. In both of these, Central and Central—West seem to be at one level and Central—East at a substantially lower level.

One cannot help but be struck by the fact that Central—East, an area so similar in its general characteristics to the other Central areas, has a homicide rate (albeit third highest in the county) which is so much lower than its sister areas. The data in Table 81 shows that the marked differentiation of Central—East from Central and Central—West appears also in many of the other social indices—*most* notably in income and other indicators of economic status, education, percentage of owner-occupied homes, illegitimate birthrate and health. This serves not only to explain the sharp differences in homicide rate but to lend strength to the assumption, which underlies this study, that homicide is a social phenomenon related to other social phenomena.

Chapter V

SUMMARY

Earlier the social planning areas (on a table and a map) were arranged according to quintile ranks in homicide rate. Those ranks with the quintile ranks are now compared on a comprehensive pair of indices: "Social problems" and "area characteristics" which are computed on the basis of the various socio-economic indices previously considered and graphed.

The table indicates that in the first homicide quintile the quintile-rank correlation is almost perfect. In the second and subsequent homicide quintiles it is discernible but far less conclusive.

TABLE 82

COMPARISON OF SOCIAL PROBLEMS AND AREA CHARACTERISTICS WITH HOMICIDE RATE RANKS BY QUINTILES OF THE SOCIAL PLANNING AREAS

	Quintile Ranks[40]		
Social Planning Areas[41]	Homicide Rate	Social Problems	Area Characteristics
Central—West	1	1	1
Central	1	1	1
Central—East	1	1	1
Kinsman	1	1	1
Goodrich	1	1	2
Downtown*	--	--	--
North Broadway	1	2	2
Hough	1	1	1
Glenville	2	2	2
Mount Pleasant	2	2	3
University	2	2	1
Norwood	2	2	2
Clark-Fulton	2	3	2
West Side	2	3	3
Corlett	2	3	3

—(Continued)

[40]Downtown area omitted.

[41]Social problems and area characteristics are ranked from area of greatest need to area of least need; homicide rate is ranked from highest to lowest.

182   *HOMICIDE IN AN URBAN COMMUNITY*

TABLE 82 (Continued)

COMPARISON OF SOCIAL PROBLEMS AND AREA CHARACTERISTICS WITH HOMICIDE RATE
RANKS BY QUINTILES OF THE SOCIAL PLANNING AREAS

	Social Planning Areas[41]		
Quintile Ranks[40]	*Homicide Rate*	*Social Problems*	*Area Characteristics*
Near West Side	2	1	1
Euclid	2	4	5
North Collinwood	2	4	3
Lee-Miles	3	2	4
Tremont	3	1	1
Chagrin Valley	3	5	5
South Brooklyn	3	4	4
Jefferson	3	5	4
Parma-South	3	3	5
Woodland Hills	3	3	3
Puritas-Bellaire	3	3	2
Fairview-Olmsted	4	5	5
South Broadway	4	2	2
West Shore	4	5	5
Cleveland-University Heights	4	5	5
Denison	4	3	2
South Euclid-Lyndhurst	4	5	5
Shaker-Beechwood	4	5	5
South Collinwood	4	3	3
East Cleveland	4	4	3
Southwest County	5	4	3
Lakewood	5	5	3
Garfield	5	4	4
Cuyahoga Valley	5	3	4
Bedford-Maple Heights	5	2	4
Riverside	5	4	4
Edgewater	5	4	2

The extremely homicidal areas are most important, however. The five areas with the highest rate (Central—West, Central, Central—East, Kinsman, and Goodrich) account for 397 of the 595 assailants whose residences are known. Their *ranks* in homicide rate are as follows:[42]

Area	*Rank*
Central-West	41
Central	40
Central-East	39
Kinsman	38
Goodrich	37

---

[42]If Downtown were included, these would be 42 areas, and each of these areas would be one rank higher than as listed here.

HOMICIDE IN AN URBAN COMMUNITY 183

It is interesting to summarize the ranking of these five areas in the nine social indices already graphed and tabulated.

TABLE 83

	Area				
Index	*Central— West*	*Central*	*Central— East*	*Kinsman*	*Goodrich*
Socio-economic status	39	41	36	40	38
Undesirable neighborhood conditions	40	39	37	38	41
Financial Dependency	41	40	39	38	37
Space	41	40	38	39	35
Crowded Housing Conditions	40	41	39	38	37
Stability of Population	41	40	37	35	36
Social Maladjustment	41	40	39	38	37
Family and Individual Adjustment Problems	41	38	39	40	35
Ill Health	40	41	39	36	37
Average Rank in the 9 Indices	40.44	40.0	38.11	38.0	37.0

The result is quite impressive. Whereas the quintile averages and the graphs of the top thirteen areas were *generally* indicative of the correlation of homicide with other social problems, there were many deviations and unexpected variations to be rationalized. This in itself is not surprising. It follows from the skewness of the homicide curve—that is, from the fact that the homicides were so heavily concentrated in a few areas. To study those areas and to compare them as a group with the other areas in the county confirm the original generalizations.

184 HOMICIDE IN AN URBAN COMMUNITY

The five areas with the highest rate of homicide rank as the top five in nearly every index of social need and maladjustment. They never rank below the top seven. In financial dependency and social maladjustment the correlation with homicide rate is perfect and positive.

TABLE 84

Area[43]	Rank in Homicide Rate	Rank in Financial Dependency	Rank in Social Maladjustment
Central-West	41	41	41
Central	40	40	40
Central-East	39	39	39
Kinsman	38	38	38
Goodrich	37	37	37

The average standing of each of the five areas in the nine indices reveals a steady progression coinciding (though by no means proportionate) with the progression in homicide rate.

It can safely be generalized, therefore, that the areas with the very highest homicide rates are the areas with the lowest socio-economic status, the most undesirable neighborhood conditions, the greatest financial dependency, the most acute problems of space and crowded housing conditions, the least stability of population, the greatest social maladjustment and family and individual adjustment problems, and the poorest health.

No one social trait can be labeled as *the* cause of homicide. But the relation of undersirable social conditions in general to high homicide rates leads inescapably to the conclusion that there is more than a chance relationship.

Homicide is not accidental. Nor is the fact that some areas have a high rate and others a low rate a matter of coincidence. The almost invariable association of a high homicide rate with so many other symptoms of social ill-health and economic need shows almost conclusively the socio-economic basis of homicide. This conclusion

[43]Downtown area is omitted.

and the facts on which it is based may point the way to an intensification of the long-range efforts for slum eradication, better housing, more universal education, and better work opportunities. Homicide will not be eliminated in this way, but it will be dramatically reduced. On the basis of this social study, one may say that even more than human happiness and welfare is at stake; it is literally a matter of life and death.

Appendix A

THE CENSUS TRACTS INCLUDED IN THE SOCIAL PLANNING AREAS OF CUYAHOGA COUNTY

Cleveland

Social Planning Area	Census Tracts Included
1. Central	L-9; M-7 to M-9; N-2
2. Central—East	M-1 to M-6; N-1
3. Central—West	G-9; H-7 to H-9; I-1 to I-9; J-1 to J-3
4. Clark-Fulton	B-7 to B-9; E-1 to E-3
5. Corlett	O-6; T-1; T-3 to T-5; T-9; U-1 to U-4
6. Denison	D-9; E-4 to E-6
7. Downtown	G-1 to G-3; G-6 to G-8
8. Edgewater	A-1; A-3
9. Glenville	K-4; P-1 to P-8; R-1 to R-5
10. Goodrich	G-4, G-5; H-1 to H-6; K-1
11. Hough	L-1 to L-8; R-6, R-9
12. Jefferson	A-4; B-1; W-3, W-5, W-9; X-1
13. Kinsman	N-3, N-4, N-6 to N-8
14. Lee-Miles	U-5 to U-9; V-1 to V-3
15. Mount Pleasant	S-8, S-9; T-6 to T-8
16. Near West Side	A-2, A-8, A-9; B-5, B-6; C-1 to C-9
17. North Broadway	J-4 to J-8; N-9
18. North Collinwood	Q-1, Q-2, Q-6, Q-7
19. Norwood	K-2, K-3, K-5 to K-9
20. Puritas-Bellaire	X-2 to X-6
21. Riverside	W-1, W-2, W-4; W-6 to W-8
22. South Broadway	J-9; O-1 to O-5; O-7 to O-9
23. South Brooklyn	F-1 to F-7; E-7 to E-9
24. South Collinwood	P-9; Q-3 to Q-5; Q-8, Q-9; Z-1
25. Tremont	D-1 to D-8
26. University	R-7, R-8; S-1, S-2
27. Westside	A-5 to A-7; B-2 to B-4
28. Woodland Hills	N-5; S-3 to S-7; T-2

HOMICIDE IN AN URBAN COMMUNITY

The Suburbs

29. Bedford-Maple Heights
    Bedford .... BD-1 to BD-3
    Bedford Heights CC-36
    Glen Willow CC-51
    Maple Heights MH-1, MH-2
    Oakwood CC-40
    Walton Hills CC-41
30. Chagrin Valley
    Bentleyville CC-53
    Chagrin Falls Twp. CC-54
    Chagrin Falls Village CC-55
    Gates Mills CC-45
    Hunting Valley CC-47
    Moreland Hills CC-52
    Orange CC-49
    Pepper Pike CC-46
    Solon CC-50
    Woodmere CC-48
31. Cleveland-University Heights
    Cleveland Heights .... CH-1 to CH-17
    University Heights UH-1
32. Cuyahoga Valley
    Brecksville CC-27
    Broadview Heights CC-26
    Independence CC-25
    Valley View CC-29
33. East Cleveland .... EC-1 to EC-10
34. Euclid .... EU-1 to EU-7
35. Fairview-Olmsted
    Fairview Park FP-1
    North Olmsted NO-1, NO-2
    Olmsted Twp. CC-5
    Olmsted Falls CC-6
    Parkview CC-9
    Riveredge Twp. CC-10
    West View CC-7
36. Garfield
    Cuyahoga Heights CC-22
    Garfield Heights .... GH-1 to GH-7

HOMICIDE IN AN URBAN COMMUNITY

	Newburgh Heights	CC-20, CC-21
37.	Lakewood	LW-1 to LW-18
38.	Parma South	
	Brooklyn	BK-1
	Brooklyn Heights	CC-23
	Linndale	CC-15
	North Royalton	CC-18, CC-19
	Parma	PR-1 to PR-6
	Parma Heights	CC-17
	Seven Hills	CC-24
39.	Shaker-Beechwood	
	Beechwood	CC-35
	North Randall	CC-38
	Shaker Heights	SH-1 to SH-6
	Warrensville Heights	CC-37
	Warrensville Twp.	CC-39
40.	South Euclid-Lyndhurst	
	Bratenahl	CC-28
	Highland Heights	CC-42
	Lyndhurst	LH-1
	Mayfield Heights	MY-1
	Mayfield	CC-43
	Richmond Heights	CC-30
	South Euclid	SE-1, SE-2
41.	Southwest County	
	Berea	BE-1 to BE-3
	Brookpark	CC-11
	Middleburgh Heights	CC-12
	Strongsville	CC-13, CC-14
42.	West Shore	
	Bay	BA-1
	Rocky River	RR-1, RR-2
	Westlake	CC-2

INDEX

Aid for the aged, 145-146
Alcohol, presence of
  felonious homicides, 92-94
  justifiable homicides, 95-97
Areas of homicides
  concentration of, 105-106
  distribution of, 105-106
  three highest compared, 177-180
  undesirable conditions, 163

Children accepted for service, 148-149

Dwellings
  age, 138

Education, 125-128
  significance of slightly higher education, 127-128

Family and individual adjustment, 173
Felony
  killing while perpetrating felony, 26-29
Financial dependency, 164

Homicide rate, 112-113
  other social indicators, 158
  procedure for comparison, 158-160
Homicides
  all types
    days, 8-10
    hours, 11
    months, 7-8
    number of, 5
    years, 7
  causes complex, 184-185
  classification, 5-7
  felonious (for specific felonious homicides, *see* Murder in the First Degree, etc.)
  ages of persons charged with, 70-71
  assailants, number of, 14
  conflicts culminating in, types, 72-77
  conviction statistics, summary of, 19
  definition of, 5-7

disposition of specific felonious homicides (*see* also Murder in the First Degree; Murder in the Second Degree; Manslaughter in the First Degree), 21-40
felony murders, 26-29
grand jury; failure to indict, 16
guilty, 17
  number pleading, 18
insane, number of accused persons, 17
manslaughter in the first degree. *See* this separate title.
murder in the first degree. *See* this separate title.
murder in the second degree. *See* this separate title.
nolle prosequi, cases resulting in, 16
not guilty, 17
number of, 14
preliminary examination, number discharged upon, 14
probation, 19
race. *See* Race—Felonious Homicides
trial by court or jury, 18-19
victims, number of, 14
justifiable
  ages of decedents, 81-82
  definition of, 78
  number, 79
    police officers, cases involving, 80-81
    private persons, cases involving, 79-80
  police officers, cases involving, 80-81
  private persons, cases involving, 79-80
  race, 79-80, 81
  type homicide situations, 80, 81
  racial and ethnic distribution, 113-118
  summary of statistics, 98-100
Housing, crowded conditions, 167

Ill health, 174
Illegitimate birthrate, 151

192 HOMICIDE IN AN URBAN COMMUNITY

Income
    downtown and university areas unique, 119
    median family, 119-122
    significance of small differences, 122
Infant mortality, 155

Juvenile delinquency, 152-154

Manslaughter in the first degree
    definition of, 35
    disposition other than by trial or upon a plea of guilty, 37
    grand jury; failure to indict, 37
    guilty, 37-39
      as charged, 38
      lesser offense, 37-38
      number pleading, 38
    nolle prosequi, disposition by, 37
    not guilty, 38
    number charged with, 37
    preliminary examination, accused discharged upon, 37
    probation, 39-40
    race. *See* Race—Felonious Homicides
    summary of conviction statistics, 39
    trial by court or jury, 39
Married couples with no household, 143
    significance in homicide rate, 143
Murder in the first degree
    definition of, 21-22
    disposition other than by trial or upon a plea of guilty, 22-24
    felony murders, 26-29
    grand jury; failure to indict, 22
    guilty, 24
      as charged, 24
      lesser offense, 24
      number pleading, 24
    insane, number of accused persons, 22-24
    mercy, recommendation of, 26
    not guilty, 24
    number charged with, 22
    probation, 29
    race. *See* Race—Felonious Homicides
    summary of conviction statistics, 24-25
    trial by court or jury, 25-26
Murder in the second degree
    definition of, 29

    disposition other than by trial or upon a plea of guilty, 31
    grand jury; failure to indict, 31
    guilty, 31-32
      as charged, 31
      lesser offense, 31-32
      number pleading guilty, 32
      insane, number of accused persons, 31
    not guilty, 31
      by reason of insanity, 31
    number charged with, 29-31
    probation, 34-35
    race. *See* Race—Felonious Homicides
    summary of conviction statistics, 32
    trial by court or jury, 33

Neglect and dependency complaints, 152-153
Negro (*see also* Race and Race subtitle under other Sections)
    significance in homicide areas, 177
Neighborhood, undesirable conditions, 163

Occupation
    distribution, 128-131
Overcrowded housing, 135
    homicide rate significance, 135
Owner-occupied dwellings, 140
    insignificance in homicide rate, 140

Police
    apprehension of assailants; record, 12-13
    justifiable homicides, police officers as slayers, 80-81
Population density, 131-133
    homicide rate significance, 133
    net acres, 131
Population stability, 170
Public assistance cases, 148

Quintile maps deceptive, 106-112

Race—felonious homicides
    accused persons; total number and percent, 41-42
    manslaughter in the first degree, 47-49
      accused persons; percentages, 47
      conviction statistics, comparison of, 47-48

HOMICIDE IN AN URBAN COMMUNITY

probation, 49
trial by court or jury, 48-49
murder in the first degree, 42-45
accused persons; percentages, 42-43
conviction statistics, comparison of,
42-44
mercy, recommendation of, 44-45
probation, 45
trial by court or jury, 44
murder in the second degree, 46-47
accused persons; percentages, 46
conviction statistics, comparison of,
46
probation, 47
trial by court or jury, 46-47
negro killing white, 51-54
sex. *See* Sex—Felonious Homicides
summary of statistics, 54-56
white killing negro, 51-54
Race—justifiable homicides
decedents, races of, 79-81
sex. *See* Sex—Justifiable Homicides
slayers, races of, 79-81

Sex—felonious homicides
comparison of female and male conviction statistics, 63
comparison of male-killing-male with
male-killing-female statistics, 68-69
females
accused, number, 57-58
killing females, 60-62
killing males, 57-60

probation, 59, 60, 61, 62, 63
race; defendants and victims, 59-61
probation, 60, 61, 63
males killing females, 64-69
probation, 67, 68, 69
race; defendants and victims, 67-68
probation, 68
weapons, choice of. *See* Weapons
Sex—justifiable homicides
police officers, cases involving, 80
private persons, cases involving, 80
weapons, choice of. *See* Weapons
Social and economic factors
summary and conclusion, 181-185
Social maladjustment, 171
Social planning areas
census tracts included, 187-189
Socio-economic status, 161
Space, 166
Substandard housing, 138
homicide rate significance, 138-140

Time of homicides. *See* Homicides
Tuberculosis, 155

Weapons
homicides other than justifiable, 83
race differences, 83-88
sex differences, 88
justifiable homicides
cases involving police officers, 91
cases involving private persons, 88
race differences, 88-90
sex differences, 91